EU LAW

WITHDRAWN

CHRIS TURNER

HODDER
EDUCATION
AN HACHETTE UK COMPANY

Orders: please contact Bookpoint Ltd, 130 Milton Park, Abingdon, Oxon OX14 4SB.
Telephone: (44) 01235 827720. Fax: (44) 01235 400454. Lines are open from
9.00 – 5.00, Monday to Saturday, with a 24 hour message answering service.
You can also order through our website www.hoddereducation.co.uk

If you have any comments to make about this, or any of our other titles, please send
them to educationenquiries@hodder.co.uk

British Library Cataloguing in Publication Data
A catalogue record for this title is available from the British Library

ISBN 978 0 340 92679 6

This edition published 2006
Impression number   10 9 8 7 6 5 4
Year   2009

Hachette UK's policy is to use papers that are natural, renewable and recyclable
products and made from wood grown in sustainable forests. The logging and
manufacturing processes are expected to conform to the environmental regulations of
the country of origin.

Typeset by Transet Limited, Coventry, England.
Printed in Great Britain for Hodder Education, an Hachette UK Company,
338 Euston Road, London NW1 3BH by CPI Cox & Wyman, Reading, RG1 8EX.

CONTENTS

TABLE OF CASES

PREFACE

The Key Cases series is designed to give a clear understanding of important cases. This is useful when studying a new topic and invaluable as a revision aid.

Each case is broken down into fact and law. In addition many cases are extended by the use of important extracts from the judgment or by comment or by highlighting problems. In some instances students are reminded that there is a link to other cases or material. If the link case is in another part of the same Key Cases book, the reference will be clearly shown. Some links will be to additional cases or materials that do not feature in the book.

To give a clear layout, symbols have been used at the start of each component of the case. The symbols are:

 Key Facts – These are the basic facts of the case.

 Key Law – This is the major principle of law in the case, the *ratio decidendi*.

 Key Judgment – This is an actual extract from a judgment made on the case.

 Key Comment – Influential or appropriate comments made on the case.

 Key Problem – Apparent inconsistencies or difficulties in the law.

 Key Link – This indicates other cases which should be considered with this case.

The Key Link symbol alerts readers to links within the book and also to cases and other material especially statutory provisions which is not included.

At the start of each chapter there are mind maps highlighting the main cases and points of law. In addition, within most chapters, one or two of the most important cases are boxed to identify them and stress their importance.

Each Key Case book can be used in conjunction with the Key Facts book on the same subject. Equally they can be used as additional material to support any other textbook.

The Key Cases book on EU Law starts with cases on general principles then covers the main cases on enforcement, Article 234 references, supremacy and direct effect, on the four freedoms, competition law and discrimination and social policy.

The law is as I believe it to be on 1 March 2006.

Chris Turner

CHAPTER 1

SOURCES OF LAW – GENERAL PRINCIPLES OF LAW

1.1 Proportionality

 Italy v Watson and Belmann 118/75 [1976] ECR 1185

A young English woman had settled in Italy with her Italian boyfriend but without obtaining the necessary work permit. When they split and the boyfriend reported her to Italian immigration authorities the penalty under Italian law was deportation.

The ECJ held that, while the Italian State was clearly entitled to insist on procedures for entry within the scope of Directive 68/360 and to impose sanctions, its action was disproportionate to the required objective. The woman's Art 39 rights had been infringed.

R v Pieck 157/79 [1980] ECR 2171 p 69 which makes the same point on refusal of entry.

 R v Intervention Board, ex p Man (Sugar) Ltd
181/84 [1985] ECR 2889

A sugar trader failed to apply for the necessary export licenses by the time specified. The bank where securities had to be

lodged acted in accordance with Regulation 1880/83 and
forfeited the securities, resulting in a loss of £1,670 to the
trader. In the Art 234 reference the trader's argument that the
forfeiture procedure was disproportionate was accepted.

The ECJ, in its preliminary ruling, identified that the licensing
requirement under the Regulation was only for the purpose of
ensuring sound management of the market. On this basis the
total forfeiture provided for by the Regulation was
disproportionate to the actual offence committed by the trader
and was not valid according to the court.

The ECJ applies the principle both to national legislation
introducing EC measures and to EC legislation in either
instance by determining whether the legislation goes beyond
what is necessary to achieve the actual purpose in the Treaty.

1.2 Equality

ECJ *P v S and Cornwall County Council*
C-13/94 [1996] All ER (EC) 397

A male employee of a college informed the Director of Studies
that he was undergoing 'gender reassignment'. He began
dressing as a woman and was then dismissed after undergoing
some surgery. He brought an action for sex discrimination. In
the reference the ECJ agreed.

The ECJ took a broad view of sex discrimination and applied
the principle of equality to the dismissal of a transsexual.

In *Grant v South Western Trains Ltd* (1998) the court did not feel bound to apply the same principle of equality to same sex couples. This was because the regulations applied equally whatever the relationship, man and man or woman and woman. However, this position is now changed under the Framework Directive.

Prais v The Council 130/75 [1976] ECR 1589 p 128

1.3 Legal certainty

ECJ **Mulder v Minister of Agriculture and Fisheries**
120/86 [1988] ECR 2321

A dairy farmer entered into an agreement not to supply milk for five years in return for a payment. A regulation on milk quotas was then introduced while the agreement was still in force. The quota system contained no measures for farmers who were part of the agreement, as a result of which the farmer was prevented from supplying milk when his agreement ended. The reference to the ECJ confirmed that his rights were being infringed.

The ECJ held that the farmer must be entitled to resume production and supply at the end of the agreement. He had a legitimate expectation based on the legal certainty of the agreement. He had legitimate expectations based on the agreement he had made in good faith.

CFI *R v Ministry of Agriculture, Fisheries and Food, ex p Hamble (Offshore) Fisheries Ltd* [1995] 2 All ER 714

The Ministry introduced a stringent system for granting fishing licences so as to protect fish stocks in UK waters which had become overworked. The reference confirmed that the claimant's action could not succeed.

The Court of First Instance held that the principle of legitimate expectations could not apply and the rights of the holders of fishing licences were not infringed by the arrangements. This was because arrangements of this type must be allowed to cater for changes in circumstances and reduced fish stocks was a significant change in circumstances.

'The principles of legal certainty and the protection of legitimate expectation are fundamental to European Community law. Yet these principles are merely general maxims derived from the notion that the Community is based on the rule of law and can be applied to individual cases only if expressed in enforceable rules ... other principles ... run counter to legal certainty and ... the right balance will need to be struck'.

1.4 Natural justice

ECJ *Union Nationale des Etraineurs et Cadres Techniques Professionels du Football (UNECTEF) v Heylens* 226/86 [1987] ECR 4097

A Belgian football trainer possessed a Belgian diploma but was denied the right to take up training in France. He was not given any hearing nor was any reason given for the decision. The reference identified that his rights under Art 39 had been infringed.

In the reference the ECJ held that this was a breach of process. Member States must provide both a proper hearing and a right to appeal.

The court stated that: '[in] a question of securing the effective protection of a fundamental right conferred by the Treaty on Community workers [they] must be able to defend that right under the best possible conditions and have the possibility of deciding, with a full knowledge of the relevant facts, whether there is any point in applying to the courts'.

Bosman v Royal Belgian Football Association and EUFA C-415/93 [1995] ECR I-4921 p 74

1.5 Protection of fundamental human rights

ECJ *J. Nold KG v Commission* 4/73 [1974] ECR 491

A coal wholesaler challenged a decision issued by the Commission under the ECSC Treaty that it could not comply with and that it claimed would undermine its right to freely pursue its business activities which it in turn claimed was a breach of fundamental human rights guaranteed by the German constitution.

The ECJ rejected the claim on the basis that the wholesaler was not being discriminated against since it was being treated no differently from other undertakings that also could not comply. However, it also stated that fundamental human rights form an integral part of the general principles of law that must be observed.

The Court stated that in safeguarding such rights it was bound to draw inspiration from constitutional traditions common to the Member States, and ... cannot therefore uphold measures which are incompatible ... Similarly, international Treaties for the protection of human rights ... of which they are signatories, can supply guidelines which should be followed'.

Now the amended Art 6 in any case guarantees human rights:

'(1) The Union is founded on the principles of liberty, democracy, respect for human rights and fundamental freedoms, and the rule of law, principles which are common to the member states.
(2) The Union shall respect fundamental rights as guaranteed by the European Convention for the Protection of Human Rights and Fundamental Freedoms signed in Rome on 4 November 1950 and as they result from the constitutional traditions common to the member states, as general principles of Community law'.

CHAPTER 2

ENFORCEMENT OF EU LAW

Art 226 Actions against Member States

Commission v Belgium (1970)
Liability arises whenever any state body fails to fulfil its obligations

Art 230 Actions against institutions for exceeding their powers

Plaumann v Commission (1963)
Individual concern means that the decision affects the body because of attributes it has
International Fruit Co. v Commission (1971)
A Regulation may be challenged if it has no general application but is a 'bundle of individual Decisions'

ENFORCEMENT (DIRECT ACTIONS)

Art 232 Actions against institutions for failing to act

Parliament v Council (1987)
Art 232 is applied where the applicant can show that they were entitled to a decision and none was actually addressed to them or an action has not been taken which is of direct and individual concern to them

Art 288 Actions for damages against institutions

Zuckerfabrik Schoppenstedt v Council (1971)
- there must be a legislative measure which involves choices of economic policy
- and this must involve a breach of a superior rule of law
- which is sufficiently serious
- and the superior rule is of a type which was for the protection of individuals
- and only if all parts are satisfied can fault be shown

2.1 Actions against Member States under Art 226 and Art 227

 ECJ *Commission v Belgium* 77/69 [1970] ECR 237

Belgium had breached Art 90 (ex Art 95) by a discriminatory tax on wood. The Belgian Government argued that an amendment was actually put before its Parliament but never gained force because Parliament was dissolved in the meantime. It argued that, since it was prevented from legislating, the breach was beyond its control.

The ECJ would not accept this reasoning and held that 'liability under [Art 226] arises whatever the agency of the State whose action or inaction is the cause of the failure to fulfill its obligations'.

2.2 Actions against the institutions under Art 230 for exceeding their powers

ECJ *Plaumann v Commission* 25/62 [1963] ECR 95

 German importers, including Plaumann, complained that a refusal by the Commission to suspend customs duties on mandarin oranges and tangerines exceeded its powers. Their argument failed when it was shown that any individual in Germany might have imported the fruit so they could not show 'individual concern'.

 It was held that in order for a private applicant to claim under Art 230 individual concern must be shown and this means that the decision or Regulation must affect the applicant.

 The court held that this would be 'by reason of certain attributes which are peculiar to them or by reason of circumstances in which they are differentiated from all other persons and by virtue of these factors distinguishes them individually just as in the case of the person addressed'.

 Töepfer v Commission 106 &107/63 [1965] ECR 405 which slightly modifies this.

ECJ *International Fruit Co v Commission* 41-44/70 [1971] ECR 411

A decision only applied to a limited number of importers who had been granted licenses before a specific date. The issue was whether the importers had *locus standi* to challenge the decision.

The ECJ held that there will be individual concern and therefore *locus standi* is possible if there is a 'closed group' of people affected by the decision. In the case there was such a 'closed group' because of the limited number of importers.

The Court stated that a Regulation can only be challenged when it is not one having general application within the meaning given in Art 249 but is instead 'a bundle of individual Decisions taken by the Commission, each of which, although taken in the form of a Regulation, affected the legal position of the applicant'.

Unión de Pequenos Agricultores (UPA) v Council
C-50/00 [2003] QB 893

A trade association unsuccessfully challenged a Regulation in the CFI as it could not show individual concern. The CFI stated that it could have brought an action instead in the national court and then asked for an Art 234 reference. The case went on to the ECJ.

The Advocate-General, in his reasoned opinion, stated that a challenge under Art 230 was a more appropriate procedure and acknowledged the inherent difficulties in trying to follow the route recommended by the CFI. A national court would not have the power to annul the measure and so could only consider whether there was enough doubt as to its legality to justify a reference being made. Also certain measures would not give rise to actions in national courts, so could not be challenged by individuals. He also felt the definition of individual concern was too restrictive and that there was no reason why an individual should have to show a difference from other individuals affected by the measure. He preferred a test based on an individual having suffered a substantial adverse affect because of his particular circumstances. Nevertheless, the ECJ confirmed the *Plaumann* (1963) test.

Quere et Cie v Commission T-177/01 [2003] QB 854 where between the Advocate-General's opinion and the ECJ ruling in UPA the CFI suggested a different test based on the Advocate-General's opinion in UPA. There would be individual concern if the measure: 'affects his legal position in a manner which is both definite and immediate, by restricting his rights or imposing obligations on him'.

The result is that there is unlikely to be any change to the definition now without amendment to the Treaty.

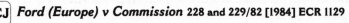

CJ *Ford (Europe) v Commission* 228 and 229/82 [1984] ECR 1129

Ford challenged an interim decision by the Commission on Ford's ban on selling right hand drive Ford vehicles to dealers in Germany.

The ECJ held that a challenge was possible because the Commission had no power to make interim decisions.

This suggests that it is probably easier for Art 230 to be used in respect of powers that are not possessed at all by the institution challenged in the application than where powers are simply abused.

CJ *Transocean Marine Paint Association v Commission* 17/74 [1975] 2 CMLR D75

The Association had enjoyed an exemption from Art 81 for 10 years when the Commission unilaterally reviewed the exemption and imposed entirely new conditions.

The Court held that the Commission had acted in breach of a general right to be heard, and of the general principle of legal certainty. Its act was thus invalid.

The ground allows the ECJ to review how the acts of the institutions conform to EC law. As this includes the general principles any violation of EC law of any type may be declared invalid.

 Werner A. Bock KG v Commission (the Chinese Mushrooms case) 62/70 [1971] ECR 897

A firm applied to import Chinese mushrooms into Germany. Since the mushrooms were freely available in the EC at the time, the German Government needed authority from the Commission if it wished to prohibit the import. The Commission issued a decision allowing the import ban.

The ECJ decided that the import ban lacked proportionality but also considered the question of misuse of power by the Commission and held that there was evidence of collaboration between the Commission and the German Government in the issuing of the decision so that there was a misuse of power. The Commission used its power to issue decisions, a power that it does in fact possess, but did so for an objective that was contrary to what it was given for and the decision was invalid.

2.3 Actions against the institutions under Art 232 for a failure to act

 Parliament v Council 13/83 [1987] ECR 1513

This involved a challenge by Parliament over an alleged failure by the Council to ensure (i) freedom to provide international transport and (ii) to establish the conditions in which non-resident transporters were able to operate in other Member States.

The Court accepted this as an appropriate ground for review and identified that Art 232 is appropriate where the applicant can show that they were entitled to a decision and none was actually addressed to them or where an action has not been taken which is of direct and individual concern to them. The Court held that the Council had failed on the second count because it involved a legally perfect obligation which should have been implemented within the transitional period. It did not accept the first count because it was too imprecise. However, the case has subsequently led to development of an EC transport policy.

There are no clear guidelines on when Art 232 actions are appropriate. However, generally if there is a result to be achieved and an obligation is sufficiently well defined then any attempt to disregard it will fall within the scope of an Art 232 action.

2.4 Actions for damages against the institutions under Art 288

ECJ *Zuckerfabrik Schoppenstedt v Council*
5/71 [1971] ECR 975

A Regulation laid down measures to offset the differences between national sugar prices and Community reference prices that were applicable from a particular date. The applicant complained that the criteria were in fact erroneous and had caused him loss.

The applicant failed in his complaint since the Court held that the Community will not incur liability for a legislative measure that involves choices of economic policy unless there has been a breach of a superior rule of law for the protection of individuals. The ECJ also laid down criteria for determining fault (the so-called 'Schoppenstedt formula'):

- there must be a legislative measure which involves choices of economic policy;
- and this must involve a breach of a superior rule of law;
- which is sufficiently serious;
- and the superior rule is of a type which was for the protection of individuals;
- and only if all parts are satisfied will fault be shown.

There are three elements required for a successful claim:

- damage suffered by the applicant;

- fault on the part of the institution complained about;
- a causal connection between the measure complained of and the damage suffered.

 Adams v Commission 145/83 [1985] ECR 3539 where the applicant's wife hanged herself when he was arrested for industrial espionage and this was accepted as recoverable damage.

The meaning of 'court or tribunal'
Broekmeulen v Huisarts Registratie Commissie (1981)
The ECJ applies a 'functionalist' rather than a 'literalist' test

Inadmissible references
Foglia v Novello (1981)
Reference must involve genuine issue of EC law; and will genuinely assist national court to make a judgment; but cannot use to merely test the law or to delay the case

Art 234 References

References challenging the validity of EU law
R (on the application of British American Tobacco) v Secretary of State for Health (2003)
The fact that a Directive is issued under an inappropriate Treaty Article need not affect its validity

Mandatory and discretionary references
CILFIT Srl v Ministero della Sanita (1982)
A reference is not necessary: where EC law is irrelevant or peripheral; or there is an existing interpretation; or correct interpretation is so obvious that there can be no doubt

3.1 The meaning of court or tribunal

Broekmeulen v Huisarts Registratie Commissie
246/80 [1981] ECR 2311

A doctor appealed to the Appeals Committee of the Royal
Netherlands Society for the Protection of Medicine against a
decision not to register him as a GP. His appeal was based on
principles of EC Law and one issue for the ECJ was whether
the appeals committee was a 'court or tribunal' for
admissibility under the Art 234 reference procedure. Early case
law of the ECJ had laid down five criteria: statutory origin,
permanence, *inter partes* procedure, compulsory jurisdiction
and the application of rules of law, and subsequent case law
had also added independence.

Taking a functionalist rather than a literalist approach, the
ECJ held that the committee was a court for the purposes of
Art 234.

The ECJ stated 'in the practical absence of redress before the
ordinary courts ... the appeal committee which performs its
duties with the approval of the public authorities and operates
with their assistance, and whose decisions are accepted
following contentious proceedings and are in fact recognised as
final, must be deemed to be a court'.

Dorsch Consult C-54/96 [1997] ECR I-4961 which defined
and followed the functional test meaning that more bodies can
seek preliminary rulings than if a literalist test was applied.

de Coster v Collège des bourgmestre et échevins de Watermael-Boitsfort C-17/00 [2001] ECR I-9445 in which the Advocate General described the approach of the ECJ as confused.

3.2 Inadmissible references

 Foglia v Novello (No 2) **244/80 [1981] ECR 3045**

A French national ordered a consignment of Italian liqueur wine from an Italian wine merchant, Foglia, under a contract that stipulated that she should not be liable for any charges imposed by either French or Italian authorities, which would have been unlawful under EC law. The French customs did in fact impose a tax on the import which she paid and then tried to recover from the wine merchant. The Italian judge made a reference to the ECJ on the correct interpretation of Art 90.

The ECJ refused the request for a preliminary ruling on the ground that it believed that the proceedings had been initiated by the parties purely to test the validity of French tax rules.

While the decision has been criticised there is no doubt that the reference did not in fact concern an issue of EC law and therefore the reference was inappropriate.

3.3 References challenging the validity of EU law

R (on the application of British American Tobacco) v Secretary of State for Health C-491/01 [2003] All ER (EC) 604

Here BAT and Imperial Tobacco were seeking a judicial review of UK legislation which was being used to implement Directive 2001/37 into English law. The Directive concerned regulation of maximum levels of tar, nicotine and carbon monoxide in cigarettes and also health warnings and other information to be provided on individual packets of cigarettes. The basis of the application for review was, amongst other things, that there was an inappropriate legislative basis for the introduction of the Directive. The Directive had been adopted under Art 95 and Art 133.

In the reference to the ECJ, the Court held that the Directive was validly introduced under Art 95. Art 133 should not have been used but this did not affect the validity of the Directive.

3.4 Discretionary references and mandatory references

ECJ *CILFIT Srl v Ministero della Sanita*
283/81 [1982] ECR 3415

Italian wool importers challenged a rule imposing a fee for an inspection of wool imported from outside the EC as contrary to Regulation 827/68. The argument was based on a provision in the

Regulation, concerning the common organisation of the market in products listed in Annex II of the Treaty prohibiting any charges equivalent to a customs duty on imported animal products not specified or included elsewhere. The Italian Ministry of Health argued that as wool was not included in Annex II the Regulation could not apply and that the measure was so obvious as to remove any possible doubt requiring interpretation. A reference to the ECJ was made on the interpretation of paragraph 3 of Art 234, and whether the mandatory reference procedure required that a court of last resort has an absolute obligation to refer or whether it must only make a reference if it feels there is interpretative doubt.

The ECJ held that a court or tribunal against whose decisions there is no judicial remedy under national law must refer unless it has established that the question before it is irrelevant, or there is a prior interpretation, or where the correct application of Community law is so obvious that it leaves no scope for reasonable doubt.

The Court explained that it would not be necessary to refer 'if the answer to that question is not relevant, that is to say, if the answer to that question, regardless of what it might be, can in no way affect the outcome of the case' or where 'the authority of an interpretation ... already given by the Court may deprive the obligation of its purpose and thus empty it of its substance. Such [as] when the question is materially identical with a question which has already been the subject of a preliminary ruling in a similar case' or where 'the correct application of Community law may be so obvious as to leave no scope for reasonable doubt as to the manner in which the question raised is to be resolved. Before it comes to [that] conclusion the national court or tribunal must be convinced that the matter is equally obvious to the Courts of the other Member States and to the Court of Justice'.

The case has been the subject of a lot of criticism, particularly as it leaves too much discretion to the national courts and it has been said that the criteria are too easy to manipulate by the national courts and thus encourages them to decide too many difficult questions themselves thus jeopardising the uniform application of the Treaties. On the other hand it is also subject to calls for reform, particularly because of the delays caused by the backlog of cases. It is common for replies to referrals to take up to two years and in some cases there have been four year waits.

CHAPTER 4

SUPREMACY AND DIRECT EFFECT

Supremacy
Van Gend en Loos (1963)
First statement – states have given up sovereignty to new legal order
Costa v ENEL (1964)
Clear limitation of sovereign right upon which subsequent unilateral law, incompatible with aims of Community cannot prevail
International Handelsgesselschaft (1970)
Applies equally to national constitutional law
R v Secretary of State for Transport ex p Factortame (No 2) (1996)
A national court can do everything necessary to set aside national legislative provisions which might prevent Community rules from having full force and effect including temporarily suspending operation of an Act of Parliament

SUPREMACY AND DIRECT EFFECT

Direct effect
Van Gend en Loos v Nederlands Administratie der Belastingen (1963)
Measures can be enforced if clear, precise and unconditional, and conferred rights
Van Gend en Loos (1963) applies straightforwardly to substantive Treaty Articles;
Leonesio v Ministero dell'Agricoltora & delle Foreste (1972) and to regulations;
Grad v Finanzamt Traustein (1970) and decisions
Direct effect of directives
Van Duyn v Home Office (1974)
Recognised that it would be incompatible with the binding nature of a directive in Art 249 if they could not be enforced
Pubblico Ministero v Ratti (1979)
But date for implementation must have passed
Marshall v Southampton and S W Hampshire AHA (No 1) (1986)
May only be 'vertically' directly effective against the state itself
Foster v British Gas plc (1990)
Or an 'emanation of the state' (provides public service, under state control, special powers)
Indirect effect
Von Colson and Kamann v Land Nordrhein-Westfalen (1984)
Since Member States have an obligation under Art 10 to give full effect to EC law then they should interpret an improperly implemented directive so as to give effect to its objectives
State liability
Brasserie/Factortame (1996)
Can sue state for failure to implement directives if clearly gives right, breach is sufficiently serious, and the citizen suffers loss caused by the breach of EC law

4.1 The nature and effect of supremacy of EU law

ECJ *Costa v ENEL* 6/64 [1964] ECR 585

Costa, a lawyer, owned shares in a pre-privatised Italian electric company and argued that the law privatising the industry was unlawful as it contravened EC law on monopolies. The Italian Government, after a judgment by the Italian constitutional court, argued that the proceedings themselves were unlawful since the Italian court should have followed the Italian law nationalising the electric industry which came after that ratifying the Treaty.

The ECJ held that EC law took precedence over inconsistent national law, even that introduced after the signing of the Treaty.

The court stated 'By contrast with ordinary international treaties, the EC Treaty has created its own legal system which on entry into force ... became an integral part of the legal systems of the member states and which their courts are bound to apply ... the member states have limited their sovereign rights ... and have thus created a body of law which binds both their nationals and themselves.' And, on the consequences, 'The transfer, by member states from their national orders in favour of the Community order of its rights and obligations arising from the Treaty, carries with it a clear limitation of their sovereign right upon which a subsequent unilateral law, incompatible with the aims of the community cannot prevail'. 'It follows ... that the law stemming from the Treaty ... could not, because

> of its special and original nature, be overridden by
> domestic legal provisions, however framed, without
> being deprived of its character as Community law
> and without the legal basis of the Community
> itself being called into question'.

International Handelsgesellschaft GmbH v EVGF
11/70 [1970] ECR 1125

A German challenged the legitimacy of an EC Regulation
requiring export licences for agricultural products falling under
the Common Agricultural Policy (CAP). Also payment of
deposits was to be forfeited if no products were exported for
the duration of the licence. The German court agreed that the
measure was unconstitutional under German law as it
infringed basic guaranteed rights to freely run a business and
to be free of compulsory payment without proof of fault. In a
reference to the ECJ the question was whether national
constitutional law took precedence over EC law.

The ECJ held that EC law takes precedence even over the
constitutions of the Member States.

ECJ *Simmenthal SpA v Amministrazione delle Finanze dello
Stato* 70/77 [1978] ECR 1453

An Italian imported beef from France and, under Italian law
introduced in 1970, was bound to pay for inspection of the
goods at the frontier. The Italian law was inconsistent with the
requirements of Art 28 and EC Regulations of 1964 and
1968. The Italian court made an Art 234 reference to the ECJ

on the question whether it must follow the EC law or wait for the Italian law to be annulled by the Italian constitutional court according to the usual procedure.

The ECJ held that it must follow EC law in preference to any inconsistent national law.

The court stated 'directly applicable measures of the institutions ... render automatically inapplicable any conflicting provision of current national law ..., and ... also preclude the valid adoption of new national legislative measures to the extent that they would be incompatible with Community provisions ...'. As a result 'every national court must ... apply Community law in its entirety and protect rights which the latter confers on individuals and must accordingly set aside any provision of national law which may conflict with it, whether prior or subsequent to the Community rule'.

ECJ *R v Secretary of State for Transport ex p Factortame Ltd*
C-213/89 [1990] ECR I-2433

Companies registered in the UK but mostly owned by Spanish nationals were registered in the UK specifically to purchase trawlers registered in the UK. Under the Merchant Shipping Act 1988 and the Merchant Shipping (Registration of Fishing Vessels) Regulations 1988 there was a nationality requirement so that for registration a certain percentage ownership had to be in the hands of UK nationals. The applicants argued in the English court that the requirement was in breach of Art 12 in that it discriminated on nationality, as a result of which they were denied fishing rights otherwise guaranteed by EC law.

The House of Lords had to decide whether to grant an interim injunction against an Act of Parliament, enacted after membership which specifically contradicted EC law. The effect would be to suspend operation of the Act until the inconsistency issue could be settled on reference to the ECJ. As the House identified in its judgment, there was no rule in English constitutional law that would allow the injunction, nor could it see an overriding principle in EC law allowing a national court to suspend operation of a national law. In its reference the question was whether, in order to protect EC rights a national court must grant the interim suspension of an Act of Parliament. The ECJ held, to give effect to EC law, it must.

The ECJ stated 'it is for the national courts in application of the principle of co-operation laid down in Art 10 … to set aside national legislative provisions which might prevent, even temporarily, Community rules from having full force and effect' and concluded 'the full effectiveness of Community law would be just as much impaired if a rule of national law could prevent a court seized of a dispute governed by Community law from granting interim relief … It therefore follows that a court which in those circumstances would grant interim relief, if it were not for a rule of national law, is obliged to set aside that law'.

The case represents the most far reaching statement of supremacy of EC law over national law and also demonstrates quite dramatically the supranational power of the institutions of the EU.

Macarthys Ltd v Smith [1979] 1WLR 1189: contrast with the early view on membership of Lord Denning; 'if the time should ever come when our Parliament deliberately passes an Act with the intention of repudiating the Treaty or any provisions in it, or intentionally of acting inconsistently with it, and says so in express terms, then I should have thought that it would be the duty of our courts to follow the statute of our Parliament'.

4.2 Direct effect

 Van Gend en Loos v Nederlandse Administratie der Belastingen 26/62 [1963] ECR 1

 The Dutch Government reclassified import duties, increasing duty on a chemical imported from Germany and causing increased cost to a Dutch bulb grower who argued that this breached Art 25 (ex Art 12) of the Treaty. The Dutch Government challenged the right of a citizen to invoke rights granted under the treaties and in the reference the question was whether a Treaty Article could create rights which nationals could enforce in national courts.

 The Advocate-General's reasoned decision suggested that, since the Art contained no explicit mention of individual rights, it could not be construed as granting individual rights and that, if the reclassification of the duty was contrary to EC law, the appropriate action should be by Art 226 proceedings. The ECJ, however, held that, since the Treaty was clearly intended to affect individuals, although Art 25 did not mention rights, it must clearly be capable of creating rights enforceable by individuals in national courts.

 The ECJ stated 'Independently of the legislation of the member states Community law ... not only imposes obligations on individuals but is also intended to confer upon them rights which become part of their legal heritage ... not only where they are expressly granted by the Treaty, but also by reason of obligations which the Treaty imposes in a clearly defined way upon individuals ... member states and the institutions of the Community'. It added that Art 25 'contains a clear and unconditional prohibition ... ideally adapted to produce direct effects between member states and their subjects'. On Art 226 proceedings it stated 'The fact that under this Article it is the Member States who are made the subject of the negative obligation does not imply that their nationals cannot benefit from this obligation .... The fact that the Article enables the Commission and the Member States to bring before the Court a State which has not fulfilled its obligations does not mean that individuals cannot plead these obligations. [such] A restriction ... would remove all direct legal protection of the individual rights of their nationals'.

Leonesio v Ministero dell'Agricoltora & delle Foreste
93/71 [1972] ECR 287

A Regulation introduced subsidies for dairy farmers prepared
to slaughter their dairy herds in order to reduce the 'milk lake'
(over-production of milk within the Community). The
applicant had killed her cows but was then refused the
subsidies by the Italian state.

The ECJ held that the Regulation met the *Van Gend en Loos*
(1963) criteria for direct effect. It was clear and precisely
stated and was directly effective and enforceable and by the
applicant.

 Grad v Finanzamt Traustein **9/70 [1970] ECR 825**

A German company challenged a tax imposed on it, arguing
that the tax breached an EC Directive requiring amendment
to national VAT laws and of a decision which gave a time
limit for doing so.

The ECJ decided that the company was entitled to rely on the
decision provided that it satisfied the *Van Gend en Loos*
criteria.

The ECJ said it would be 'incompatible with the binding
nature of decisions … to exclude the possibility that persons
affected may [enforce them] the effectiveness of such a
measure would be weakened if … nationals … could not …

invoke it … and the national courts could not take it into consideration'.

Since decisions are binding only on the party to whom they are addressed the lack of direct applicability that occurs with directives does not apply. However, some of the problems that occur with Directives in relation to private parties could still occur if the party is not one to whom the decision is addressed.

4.3 Direct effect and Directives

ECJ *Pubblico Ministero v Ratti* 148/78 [1979] ECR 1629

Ratti was charged under Italian law for failing to properly label dangerous chemicals which he manufactured. His defence relied on two Directives requiring less stringent labelling than under Italian law. The date for implementation for one had expired without implementation but the other was still within the period.

The ECJ held that when the time limit for implementation of a Directive has passed a citizen is entitled to rely on the Directive, but where that time limit has not yet expired then the Directive cannot have direct effect. Ratti was entitled to rely on the first Directive but not the one for which the time for implementation had not yet expired.

ECJ *Marshall v Southampton and South West Hampshire AHA (No 1)* 152/84 [1986] QB 401

A woman being forced to retire by her employer complained that the different retirement ages for men and women in the UK amounted to discrimination under the 'equal access Directive', 76/207.

The ECJ confirmed that the UK law failed to fully implement the Directive and identified that the woman could only rely on the improperly implemented Directive against her employer because it was the health service, an organ of the state. The Court recognised that Directives are only capable of vertical direct effect.

The ECJ stated 'According to [Art 249] ... the binding nature of a directive ... exists only in relation to "each Member State to which it is addressed". It follows that a directive may not of itself impose obligations on an individual and that a provision of a directive may not be relied upon as such against such a person'.

HL *Duke v GEC Reliance Ltd* [1988] AC 618

On the same point as *Marshall* (1986), a woman did not wish to retire at the required age under UK law. Here, however, the woman was employed by a private company, not by the state.

The House of Lords held that it was not bound to apply Directive 76/207 because the Directive could not be effective horizontally. Even though the UK was at fault for failing to fully implement the Directive, the availability of a remedy then was entirely dependent on the identity of the employer. The House also rejected a request to apply the principle of indirect effect from *Von Colson* (1984).

The case shows that the availability of a remedy for a right given in a Directive is dependent on the nature of the party against whom the action is being brought. So it results in arbitrary justice.

ECJ *Foster v British Gas plc* C-188/89 [1990] ECR I-3313

The claimant argued that British Gas had breached Directive 76/207 by making her retire at 60 when male employees retired at 65 (legitimate under s 6(4) Sex Discrimination Act 1975, later repealed in the Sex Discrimination Act 1986). At the time of her action British Gas was not a private company but was still owned by the state.

The House of Lords, in an Art 234 reference to the ECJ, asked the question whether British Gas was a body against which the Directive could be enforced. The ECJ identified that the national courts should decide what bodies a Directive could be enforced against using vertical direct effect. It also explained that vertical direct effect can apply not only to the state itself but also to bodies that could be described as an 'emanation of the state' (or 'arm of the state') which were ones that:

- provide a public service;
- are under the control of the state;
- have powers over and above those enjoyed by private bodies.

The House of Lords determined that, at the material time (before it was privatised), British Gas was an emanation of the state.

4.4 Indirect effect

 Von Colson and Kamann v Land Nordrhein-Westfalen
14/83 [1984] ECR 1891

Joined Art 234 references involved improper implementation of Directive 76/207 by the German Government, a failure also seen in the second *Marshall* case, (*Marshall v Southampton and South West Hampshire AHA (No 2)* C-271/91 [1993] 3 CMLR 293) provision of inadequate compensation under national law by contrast to full compensation required by the Directive. Von Colson applied to work for a state body, the prison service, while Harz applied to work for a private company. Both were discriminated against contrary to the Directive.

The ECJ held that the failure of German law to provide appropriate levels of compensation amounted to incomplete implementation of the Directive. However, while a remedy would have been available to Von Colson through vertical direct effect because the employer in question was the state, Harz would have been denied a remedy because of the anomaly resulting from lack of horizontal effect. The ECJ took a novel approach in resolving this problem. It employed the obligation in Art 10 EC Treaty requiring Member States to give full effect to EC law and introduced the principle of 'indirect effect'. The German Court was bound to give full effect to the Directive and so must order full compensation in both cases.

The court stated 'Since the duty under [Art 10] to ensure fulfillment of [an] obligation was binding on all national courts ... it follows that ... courts are required to interpret their national law in the light of the wording and purpose of the Directive'.

The ECJ ignored the problems created by the absence of horizontal direct effect of Directives. It created instead a means of overcoming those problems. Nevertheless, the judgment did leave ambiguous the question of to which national law the process of indirect effect could actually apply. This then allowed the House of Lords to refuse to apply the principle in *Duke* (1988) even though it would have been a means of providing a remedy for the applicant.

ECJ **Marleasing SA v La Commercial Internacional de Alimentacion SA** C-106/89 [1990] ECR I-4135

A company argued that another company was void for lack of cause under the Spanish Civil Code. The other company sought to rely on Directive 68/151 (on company law harmonisation), which listed all the grounds for invalidating companies but did not include that ground. Spain had not implemented the Directive at all, in contrast to *Von Colson* (1984) where the Directive was improperly implemented.

In its reference the Spanish court asked the question whether the applicant could rely on the rules on the constitution of companies in Directive 68/151 since Spanish law conflicted

with the provisions of the Directive. The ECJ applied the
principles of indirect effect, held that the Spanish court was
bound to give effect to the Directive and also expanded on the
definition given in *Von Colson*.

The ECJ explained 'in applying national law, whether the
provisions concerned pre-date or post-date the Directive, the
national court asked to interpret national law is bound to do
so in every way possible in the light of the text and the aims of
the Directive to achieve the results envisaged by it'.

Marleasing (1990) increases the scope of indirect effect
significantly, and has the effect of introducing horizontal
direct effect by an indirect means, hence the title given to the
process.

4.5 State liability

ECJ *Francovich and Bonifaci v Republic of Italy*
C-6 and 9/90 [1991] ECR I-5357

Italy failed to introduce a scheme to provide a set minimum
compensation for workers on insolvency of their employers.
This breached a requirement under Directive 80/987. As a
result of the failure to properly implement the Directive the
claimants who had been made unemployed could not recover
the wages due to them.

The ECJ held that Italy was in breach of its obligations and,
since there was no other remedy available to the claimants, the

state was liable to compensate them for the loss resulting from its failure to implement the Directive. The Court introduced the principle that citizens can sue the state for non-implementation of a Directive. It also confirmed that liability was not unlimited so that three conditions must be met:

• the Directive must confer rights on individuals;
• the contents of those rights must be identifiable in the wording of the measure;
• there must be a causal link between the damage suffered and the failure to implement the Directive.

The ECJ left a number of questions unanswered and left the issue of determining the extent of liability to the national courts.

The ECJ stated 'the full effectiveness of Community rules would be impaired and the rights they recognise would be undermined if individuals were unable to recover damages where their rights were infringed by a breach of EC law attributable to a member state'.

ECJ *Brasserie du Pecheur SA v Federal Republic of Germany; R v Secretary of State for Transport, ex p Factortame Ltd (No 2)* C-46 and 48/93 [1996] ECR I-1029

In joined references one involved a German beer purity law challenged on the basis that it that was in breach of Art 28, which prohibits quantitative restrictions on imports or exports or measures having an equivalent effect. The other involved quotas under the Merchant Shipping Act 1988, challenged as breaching Art 43, rights of establishment. It also involved a breach of a previous ECJ ruling. The reference was to clarify the conditions for state liability.

The ECJ held that it was irrelevant that the breaches involved directly effective Treaty Articles and it was also irrelevant which organ of the Member State was in fact responsible for the breach. The court also redefined the conditions from *Francovich* to:

- the rule of Community law infringed must be intended to confer rights on individuals;
- the breach must be sufficiently serious to justify liability;
- there must be a direct causal link between the breach of the obligation imposed on the state and the damage actually suffered by the applicant.

 The case widens the definition of the state to include acts and omissions of any organ of the state. The scope of liability is also extended beyond directives to include any breach of Community law, regardless of whether or not it has direct effect.

 ECJ *R v HM Treasury, ex p British Telecommunications plc*
C-392/93 [1996] ECR I-1631

BT claimed that the UK Government had incorrectly implemented a Directive on public procurement in water, transport, energy and telecommunications as a result of which it suffered loss.

The ECJ agreed that the Directive was imprecisely worded so that the meaning given to it by the UK Government was in fact possible. The court also accepted that the interpretation of the Directive was shared by other Member States. There was also no ECJ case law on the Directive to direct the Member State. Because of this the Court held that the breach was not 'sufficiently serious' to justify liability, as required by the *Brasserie du Pecheur* (1996) test.

R v Ministry of Agriculture, Fisheries and Food, ex p Hedley Lomas (Ireland) Ltd C-5/94 [1996] ECR I-2553

 Dillenkofer and others v Federal Republic of Germany
C-178,179, 188, 189 and 190/94 [1996] ECR I-4845

German law was challenged for failing to properly implement the Package Holidays Directive 90/314.

The ECJ held that failure to implement a Directive by the due date is in itself a sufficiently serious breach to justify state liability and that there are situations where the seriousness of the breach is obvious so that imposition of state liability is almost a form of strict liability.

State liability diminishes the need to show direct effect or the rather strained construction of national law through indirect effect. Instead it focuses on the duty of Member State to implement EC law and attaches rigorous sanctions for failure to implement so ultimately removes any possible advantage gained by non-implementation.

4.6 Incidental horizontal effect

ECJ | *Unilever Italia SpA v Central Food SpA*
C-443/98 [2000] ECR I-7535

In a conflict over different labelling requirements the question was whether Directive 83/189 or Italian law should apply. Italy had introduced labelling requirements for geographical origin of olive oil. Under the Directive Italy should have notified the Commission of its intention to regulate. The Commission intended to regulate itself Community wide, so under the Directive Italy should not have introduced the law. Unilever supplied Central Food without the labelling required by the Italian law and then refused to pay as the labelling did not conform to Italian law. It argued that the Italian law could not apply as this would breach the Directive.

The ECJ held that the Italian law could not apply and that this did not conflict with the rules on horizontal direct effect of Directives since the Directive in this case did not involve rights on which individuals might rely. In other words the Court gave the Directive incidental horizontal effect.

➡️

CIA Security International SA v Signalson and Securitel
C-194/94 [1996] ECR I-2201 where there was no EC right being relied on, and the Directive was merely being used to disapply national law.

CHAPTER 5

ARTICLE 23–25 AND CUSTOMS TARIFFS AND ARTICLE 90 AND DISCRIMINATORY TAXATION

Commission v Italy (Re Statistical Levy) (1969)
Any pecuniary charge imposed on imports or domestic goods because they cross a frontier equivalent to a customs duty and unlawful

Art 23–25 and customs tariffs
Art 90 and discriminatory taxation

Commission v France (Reprographic Machines) (1981)
A genuine tax is a system of internal duties applied systematically to categories of products in accordance with objective criteria irrespective of origin.

5.1 Art 23–25 and customs tariffs

ECJ *Commission v Italy (Re Statistical Levy)* 24/68 [1969] ECR 193

The Italian Government levied a charge on all imports and exports in order to fund a statistical service on trade patterns. This was challenged by the Commission as being a fiscal barrier to trade.

The ECJ held that there was a breach of Art 25 and dismissed the argument that it was for the benefit of importers. Any advantage that they might gain was too uncertain and too general for the benefit to be measured. The Treaty called for the abolition of all import duties and any charges

> having an equivalent effect and the levy fell within that definition.
>
> The Court stated that 'any pecuniary charge ... which is imposed unilaterally on domestic or foreign goods by reason of the fact that they cross a frontier and which is not a customs duty in the strict sense constitutes a charge having equivalent effect within the meaning of ... the Treaty, even if it is not imposed for the benefit of the state, is not discriminatory or protective in effect'.

ECJ *Sociaal Fonds voor de Diamantarbeiders v Chougol Diamond Co* 2/69 and 3/69 [1969] ECR 211

Belgium imposed a duty on the import of uncut diamonds from South Africa. It was challenged as a breach of Art 25.

The Court held that, even though the duty was not to protect the domestic market since there are no diamond mines in Belgium, nevertheless Art 25 applied because the duty was designed to make imports more expensive.

ECJ *Kapniki Mikhailidis* C-441 and 442/98 [2000] ECR I-7415

A duty was imposed on the export of tobacco products from Greece. The argument was that the charge was justified because it was to raise money for workers in the tobacco industry.

The Court rejected the argument. There are no derogations, as there would be for Art 28 and Art 29. The only justification is where the charge is payment for services of a tangible benefit to the importer or exporter. Even then the charge must not exceed the value of the service provided.

5.2 Art 90 and discriminatory taxation

 ECJ *De Danske Bilimportorer* C-383/01 [2003] ECR I-6065

A Danish company bought and imported a new car from Germany. Danish law required all new cars to be registered and payment of a registration charge, which in this case amounted to 40,000 euros. Since the car had only cost 27,000 Euros the company claimed that there was a breach of Art 90.

The Court held that there was no breach because Denmark did not make cars so there was no similar domestic product and Art 90 only applies if the tax is discriminatory or protects domestic goods.

Article 90 allows Member States a complete discretion on imposing taxes on goods that are non-discriminatory and not for protection of domestic goods and there can be no breach if the domestic product is then more expensive. This for example results in the high taxes on cigarettes, alcohol and petrol in the UK and has led to extra work for customs trying to control people who bring in unlimited amounts with a view to commercial gain.

Commission v France (Reprographic Machines)
90/79 [1981] ECR 283

A French charge on reprographic machines was challenged by the Commission. The question for the Court was whether it was a customs duty disguised as a tax breaching Art 25 or a genuine tax falling under Art 90, if discriminatory or protectionist.

The Court held that a tax may be imposed on imported products if there is no competing domestic product as long as the tax applies to a class of product irrespective of its origin.

The Court defined a genuine tax as 'a general system of internal duties applied systematically to categories of products in accordance with objective criteria irrespective of the origin of the products'.

Commission v Luxembourg (Re Import on Gingerbread)
2/62 and 3/62 [1962] ECR 425

Luxembourg imposed a compensatory tax on imported gingerbread which it argued was introduced merely to compensate for the competitive disadvantage which resulted from a high domestic tax on one of the ingredients.

The Court held that this was in reality a customs duty disguised as a tax. Duties merely called compensatory taxes could not be allowed to stand. To do so would allow Member

States to call anything a tax and justify it by calling it compensatory when the actual effect would be to prevent genuine competition from exports.

 Humblot v Directeur des Services Fiscaux
112/84 [1987] ECR 1367

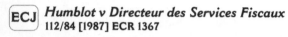

Humblot, a French national, bought and imported a Mercedes car from Germany. French road tax was charged on a sliding scale up to a certain engine capacity for which 1,000 francs was payable. For cars over this engine capacity, as the Mercedes was, there was a single charge of 5,000 francs. Humblot paid the tax but tried to reclaim it through the French courts. A reference was made.

The ECJ held that the 5,000 franc charge was excessive and, although *prima facie* non-discriminatory as it applied to all cars, in fact had the effect of discriminating against imports since France did not at the time produce cars over the set engine capacity. There was a breach of Art 90.

 Commission v France (Taxation of Spirits) 168/78 [1980] ECR 347

French law imposed significantly higher taxes on spirits distilled from cereals, such as whisky and gin, than it did on spirits distilled from fruits or grapes, such as cognac, armagnac and brandy. The first group were mostly imported and the second involved significant domestic production. As a result the Commission challenged the tax system as being contrary to Art 90. The French Government argued that the products were very different, both in taste and in the way in which they would be drunk in France i.e. the first would be diluted and often drunk as an aperitif, the latter group would be drunk neat.

The ECJ rejected the argument that there was a distinction between the grain based and fruit based drinks. It was not based on any objective justification since individuals might have widely differing drinking habits. The Court felt that it did not need to consider whether the drinks were in fact similar because it was a fact that they were in competition. Art 90(2) applied and there was a breach.

The Court held 'it is necessary to consider as "similar" products which have similar characteristics and meet the same needs [of] consumers. It is therefore necessary to determine the scope of [Art 90] on the basis not of the criterion of the strictly identical nature of the products but on that of their similar and comparable use'.

FG Roders BV C-367 to 377/93 [1995] ECR I-2229 which involved a thorough examination of the different qualities and similarities of a variety of alcoholic drinks.

CHAPTER 6

ARTICLE 28 AND FREE MOVEMENT OF GOODS

QR's and distinctly applicable MEQR's
R v Henn & Darby (1979)
A QR is an outright ban on imports
Procureur du Roi v Dassonville (1974)
All rules capable of hindering directly, indirectly, actually or potentially trade between Member States are MEQR's
Commission v Ireland (The Buy Irish Campaign case) (1983)
A measure supported by the government designed to check the flow of inter-Community trade

Art 30 derogations
R v Henn and Darby (1979)
The definition of public morality varies from state to state
R v Thompson (1979)
Public policy can include trying to protect the right to mint coinage
Campus Oil (1984)
Public security only appropriate in crisis
Commission v UK (French Turkeys) (1982)
Public health must involve a real risk to health

FREE MOVEMENT OF GOODS

Indistinctly applicable MEQR's and the 'rule of reason'
Rewe-Zentral AG v Bundesmonopolverwaltung fur Branntwein (Cassis de Dijon) (1979)
Developed the rule of reason – possible to exempt for reasons of health, consumer protection etc if necessary. Also the rule of 'mutual recognition' – if goods freely available in other Member States then no need to discriminate
Commission v Germany (The Beer Purity case) (1987)
But measure must be proportionate

Indistinctly applicable MEQR's and 'selling arrangements'
Keck and Mithouard (1993)
Application to products from other Member States of national provisions restricting or prohibiting certain selling arrangements does not hinder directly or indirectly, actually or potentially, trade between Member States – so no breach of Art 28, and *Cassis* does not apply
Vereinigte Familiapress Zeitungsverlags-und Vertriebs GmbH v Heinrich Bauer Verlag (1997)
Measures concerning something integral to the nature of the goods cannot be selling arrangements

6.1 Definitions of quantitative restrictions and measures having an equivalent effect to a quantitative restriction

ECJ *Procureur du Roi v Dassonville* 8/74 [1974] ECR 837

 A Belgian trader was prosecuted when he imported Scotch whisky from French suppliers without a certificate of origin as required by Belgian law. This was unavailable to him as it could only be issued by the UK customs authorities. He argued that the Belgian law was a breach of Art 28 and the ECJ agreed.

 The court held that the Belgian law indirectly discriminated against parties such as Dassonville, who did not import directly from Scotland but from France where the product was freely available.

 The court stated 'All trading rules enacted by Member States which are capable of hindering, directly or indirectly, actually or potentially, intra-Community trade are to be considered as measures having an equivalent effect to quantitative restrictions'.

 The case expanded on the definition provided by, the since repealed, Directive 70/50 which identified two types of MEQR:

- distinctly applicable – measures applied only to imports but not to domestic products;
- indistinctly applicable – measures applied to both but the effect on imports outweighs the general effect.

> *Geddo v Ente Nazionale Risi* 2/73 [1973] ECR 865
> which simply defines quantitative restrictions as
> 'measures which amount to a total or partial
> restraint on imports, exports or goods in transit'.

6.2 QR's and distinctly applicable MEQR's

ECJ *R v Henn and Darby* 34/79 [1979] ECR 3795

English law prohibited importing of pornography. Henn and
Darby were prosecuted, and argued that this breached Art 28.

The ECJ held that the English law, in effect an outright ban,
did amount to a quantitative restriction. However, the
derogation of public morality under Art 30 was accepted as
applying.

The ECJ held 'In principle, it is for each Member State to
determine in accordance with its own scale of values and in
the form selected by it the requirements of public morality in
its territory'.

ECJ *Commission v UK (The French Turkeys case)*
40/82 [1982] ECR 2793

A UK law banned the import of poultry. The UK
Government tried to justify the ban by arguing that it was to
prevent the spread of Newcastle Disease, a contagious
condition amongst poultry.

The ECJ accepted that the ban was imposed in the run up to Christmas for purely economic reasons, particularly at the expense of French imports. As such it was a quantitative restriction, in breach of Art 28 and the health exemption could not apply.

The court held that 'The deduction must be made that the ... measure did not form part of a seriously considered health policy [and is] a disguised restriction on imports'.

Commission v Ireland (The Buy Irish Campaign case)
249/81 [1983] ECR 4005

Ireland wished to switch 3% of consumer trade away from imports to Irish products. The Government funded the Irish Goods Council which engaged in a 'buy Irish' campaign. The Commission argued that this was a breach of Art 28.

The ECJ held that the Irish Goods Council was an organ of the state and, while it had no power to introduce binding measures it was influential on Irish traders, amounted to a distinctly applicable MEQR, and was a breach of Art 28.

The court said it was 'a programme defined by the government which affects the national economy as a whole and which is intended to check the flow of trade between Member States'.

This shows how widely the ECJ views the responsibility of the state.

 ECJ *Commission v UK (The UHT Milk case)* 124/81 [1983] ECR 203

The UK introduced an import licensing scheme. This also required retreating and repackaging imported UHT milk. The Commission challenged the measure as being in breach of Art 28.

The ECJ held that the licensing system was justified as it was necessary for regulating heat treated milk and for tracing the origins of any infection. However, the other measures were unjustified since all Member States were subject to similar controls.

 ECJ *Officiere van Justitite v Sandoz BV* 174/82 [1983] ECR 2445

Dutch authorities refused to permit the sale of muesli bars with added vitamins and imposed a licensing requirement. Their argument was that excessive consumption of vitamins was harmful to public health. However, at the time there was no medical consensus on what amounted to excessive consumption.

The ECJ held that, while the measure did appear to be a straightforward breach of Art 28, in the absence of Community harmonising measures identifying the sorts of additives that were harmful, Member States should decide the extent of the protection needed, subject to two requirements, that there should be no arbitrary discrimination and that the national measure must be proportionate to the actual risk.

6.3 Art 30 exemptions

ECJ

Conegate Ltd v Customs and Excise Commissioners
121/85 [1986] ECR 1007

A British company imported what were described as 'life size inflatable rubber love dolls'. Customs officials seized a consignment of the dolls under s 42 Customs and Consolidation Act 1976 and relied on the public morality derogation under Art 30 in a claim that the seizure amounted to a breach of Art 28.

The ECJ held that the derogation could not apply. The sale of such arts was not banned by the Act, although sale was restricted to licensed sex shops. The measure was being used as an arbitrary discrimination against imports and breached Art 28.

R v Henn and Darby 34/79 [1979] ECR 3795 p48

ECJ *R v Thompson* 7/78 [1979] ECR 2247

English law prohibited the export of coins that were no longer legal tender. Thompson and two other men were convicted of breaching this law. They argued that the coins were goods since they were no longer legal tender, and that the law thus amounted to a breach of Art 29. The UK sought to rely on the public policy exemption.

The court held that the Art 30 exemption applied as the state was protecting coinage and preventing it from being melted down.

The court stated '[the] ban ... is justified ... because it stems from the need to protect the right to mint coinage which is traditionally regarded as involving the fundamental interests of the state'.

ECJ *Campus Oil Ltd* **72/83 [1984] ECR 2727**

Irish law restricted imports of petrol in effect meaning that petrol companies had to obtain 30% of their supplies from the only Irish oil refinery located in Cork. In defence to a claim that this was a breach of Art 28, the Irish Government sought to rely on the public security defence under Art 30, the argument being that over reliance on imports could threaten the security of the state at times of shortage.

The ECJ agreed that the defence could be appropriately applied. Petrol was fundamental as an energy source and essential not only to the public but to public services also.

The ECJ held that 'the aim of ensuring a minimum supply of petroleum products at all times is to be regarded as transcending purely economic considerations and thus capable of constituting an objective covered by the concept of public security'.

 Rewe-Zentralfinanz eGmbH v Landwirtschaftskammer
4/75 [1975] ECR 843

German law required all imported apples to be subject to phyto-sanitary inspection. It claimed the exemption, protection of health and life of humans, animals and plants, in Art 30 in that it was to protect against San Jose Scale, a disease prevalent in apples.

The ECJ held that the defence could not be used since there was no similar inspection of domestically grown apples. The inspection made importing more difficult and more costly and was in effect a discrimination against imports and a breach of Art 28.

 Commission v Italy (Re export tax on art treasures)
7/68 [1968] ECR 617

Italy imposed a tax on the export of anything of an artistic, historical or archaeological nature and argued that this was necessary to protect its art treasures, a vital part of its national heritage.

The ECJ held that it was the effect of the discriminatory customs duties that was important, not its purpose. Here the effect was to hinder the export of any goods of the type identified and therefore it was a pecuniary burden and in breach.

The case actually concerned Art 25 on tariffs but illustrates the exemption of protection of national treasures.

6.4 Indistinctly applicable MEQR's and the rule of reason

 ECJ **Rewe-Zentral AG v Bundesmonopolverwaltung fur Branntwein (The Cassis de Dijon case)**
120/78 [1979] ECR 649

A German firm was prevented from importing a French blackcurrant liqueur, Cassis de Dijon. German law required such products to be a minimum alcoholic strength of 25% but the product was only 15%. The firm claimed the decision was a breach of Art 28. Germany argued that the rule was necessary to protect public health in that by keeping alcohol strengths high it would discourage increases in alcohol consumption, also that it was fair to businesses which otherwise might be subject to a commercial disadvantage because the French product was inevitably cheaper.

The ECJ laid down the 'rule of reason' that, in the case of indistinctly applicable MEQR's where a disguised discrimination was identified, Member States might justify this on grounds such as consumer protection, public health, fairness etc. It also identified a second rule of 'mutual recognition', that once goods had been lawfully produced and sold in one Member State then they should be capable of import in all other Member States. The German rules were not necessary and were disproportionate since the same object could have been achieved by clear labelling.

The Court said 'Obstacles to [free] movement resulting from disparities between the national laws relating to the marketing of the products in question must be accepted in so far as these provisions are recognised as being necessary in order to satisfy mandatory requirements relating in particular to the effectiveness of fiscal supervision, the protection of public health, the fairness of commercial transactions and the defence of the consumer'.

The 'rule of reason' applies only to indistinctly applicable MEQR's to make up for the unfairness of Art 30 exemptions not being available. Unlike those exemptions the list is non-exhaustive.

CJ

Commission v Germany (The Beer Purity case)
178/84 [1987] ECR 1227

German law required that products could only be sold as 'bier' (beer) if made from malted barley, hops, yeast and water, although there was no restriction on marketing other products. The Commission alleged that this was a disguised discrimination against imports and a breach of Art 28. Germany argued that it was necessary under the rule of reason for protection of consumers.

The ECJ recognised the heavy beer consumption of German people and that some form of protection was appropriate. However, it held that the measure taken was disproportionate since the same objective could have been achieved through careful labelling.

ECJ | ***Clinique Laboratories and Estee Lauder Cosmetics***
315/92 [1994] ECR I-317

German law prohibited the sale of cosmetics under misleading names. German authorities prohibited Estee Lauder from marketing one of its cosmetics, Clinique, on the grounds that it could mislead consumers into believing that it had medicinal properties, thus causing the company excessive costs in repackaging.

The ECJ held that there was a breach of Art 28 since the German law had a detrimental effect on imports and also was disproportionate to the objective. Estee Lauder's products were freely sold elsewhere without any confusion, and in any case in Germany they were only sold in cosmetics departments and never in pharmacies so there was no consumer protection needed.

ECJ | ***Cinethique SA v Federation Nationale des Cinemas Francaises*** 60 and 61/84 [1985] ECR 2605

French law prohibited sale or rental of films until one year after release at the cinema. Cinethique, a national video retail chain, challenged this law as being in breach of Art 28.

The ECJ held that, while the law could hinder imports, it could also be justified for encouraging cinema attendance.

The ECJ stated that 'a national system which, in order to encourage the creation of cinematographic works irrespective of their origin, gives priority, for a limited period, to the distribution of such works through the cinema is ... justified'.

ECJ *Schmidberger v Austria* C-112/00 [2003] ECR I-5659

Austrian authorities allowed a road to be closed for the purposes of a demonstration by an environmental group. The decision was challenged by transport companies as a breach of Art 28 in that it restricted trade through preventing the transport of goods.

The ECJ upheld the right of the Austrian authorities to use their discretion in such circumstances and held that to do otherwise would be to significantly undermine fundamental human rights, one aspect of which was the right to peaceful protest.

The case demonstrates a very significant application of the rule of reason and is clearly important in that fundamental human rights are a more basic right than free movement of goods.

6.5 Indistinctly applicable MEQR's and selling arrangements

ECJ *Torfaen Borough Council v B & Q plc* 145/88 [1989] ECR 3851

UK Sunday trading laws prohibited retail outlets from selling all but a small exempt range of products on Sundays. The law applied irrespective of the origin of the goods and was an 'equal burden' rule. The law led to numerous prosecutions and was challenged on the ground that it resulted in an estimated 10% reduction in trade.

The ECJ held that the rule was justified on the basis that its sole purpose was to protect 'socio-cultural' characteristics. The only requirement was that the rule should be proportionate to the objective. This was for Member States to determine.

The case led to some inconsistent application by English courts. The socio-cultural characteristics included religious observance and also the protection of shop workers who did not wish to work on Sundays. English courts held this to be disproportionate since it could be secured by employment protection laws.

B & Q plc v Shrewsbury Borough Council [1990] 3 CMLR 535; *Stoke-on-Trent City Council v B & Q plc* [1990] 3 CMLR 897

ECJ *Keck and Mithouard*
C-267 and 268/91 [1993] ECR I-6097

French law prohibited the re-sale of goods at lower than the purchase price, the justification being that it prevented large companies undercutting smaller ones and putting them at a competitive disadvantage. Keck and Mithouard were prosecuted under the law and argued that the law breached Art 28.

The ECJ identified the law as an 'equal burden' rule and introduced the concept of 'selling arrangements' which it held were not within the scope of Art 28 since they did not discriminate.

The Court said 'Such legislation may, admittedly, restrict the volume of sales … from other Member States, in so far as it deprives traders of a method of sales promotion. But the question remains whether such a possibility is sufficient to characterise the legislation in question as a measure having equivalent effect to a quantitative restriction on imports'. It added 'contrary to what has previously been decided, the application to products from other Member States of national provisions restricting or prohibiting certain selling arrangements is not such as to hinder directly or indirectly, actually or potentially, trade between Member States'.

 Keck completes the cycle and means, together with the rule of reason, indistinctly applicable MEQR's can fall within Art 28 if they are a disguised restriction on trade, have exemptions through the rule of reason that are potentially broader than Art 30, and need not lead to unnecessary litigation where they have no affect on trade.

 ECJ *Vereinigte Familiapress Zeitungsverlags-und Vertreibs GmbH v Heinrich Bauer Verlag* **C-368/95 [1997] ECR I-3689**

Austrian law prohibited the use of competitions for prizes in magazines. Familapress tried to use this law in order to prevent a German magazine from publishing a magazine containing crossword puzzles for which prizes were available.

The ECJ held that the puzzles were an integral part of the content of the goods and therefore could not fall within the rule on 'selling arrangements' in *Keck*, but instead should be consideration under Art 28 to determine if they were a breach.

CHAPTER 7

ARTICLE 39 AND THE FREE MOVEMENT OF WORKERS

Definition of worker
Levin v Staatsecretaris van Justitie (1982)
Pursuit of effective & genuine economic activity
Lawrie-Blum v Land Baden-Wurttemberg (1986)
Performs service, in return for remuneration
Steymann v Statsecretaris voor Justitie (1988)
No formal wage but involved in economic activity
R v Immigration Appeal Tribunal ex parte Antonissen (1991)
Person looking for work but not if not for a genuine reason

Workers' families
Netherlands State v Anne Florence Reed (1986)
A cohabitee is not a family member but it may infringe the worker's rights to deny him access
Centre Public d'Aide Sociale Courcelles v Lebon (1987)
Who is a dependent is a question of fact for the court to decide

FREE MOVEMENT OF WORKERS

Limitations on free movement
Van Duyn v The Home Office (1974)
Public policy or security must be exclusively on conduct of individual concerned
R v Bouchereau (1978)
And must represent a current genuine threat to society
Adoui & Cornaille v Belgium (1982)
Cannot use the exemption if the activity is not illegal in the host state
Commission v Belgium (1980)
The public service exemption applies only to civil authority or security of state

Rights of entry and residence
Procureur du Roi v Royer (1976)
Can look for work and rights of residence does not depend on permit
Equal treatment
Commission v France (Re French Merchant Seamen) (1974)
There should be no limiting on offers of employment or numbers of migrant workers
Groener v Minister for Education (1989)
Although linguistic tests are valid
Wurttembergische Milchvertung-Sudmilch A.G. v Ugliola (1969)
There should be equal conditions for nationals & migrants in pay, conditions, and dismissals
Firorini v SNCF (1975)
And families of migrant workers should enjoy the same social rights as those of host state workers
Casagrande v Landeshauptstadt Munchen (1974)
Including education

7.1 The definition of worker

ECJ *Levin v Staatsecretaris van Justitie*
53/8 [1982] ECR 1035

A British woman and her South African husband moved to the Netherlands and were financially independent. The Dutch authorities were reluctant to allow them residence so she took part-time work for a low wage, under the Dutch minimum wage, so the Dutch authorities refused to recognise her as a worker.

The ECJ would not accept that the term 'worker' could be defined quantitatively. Instead it should be measured qualitatively.

The ECJ defined work as 'the pursuit of effective and genuine activities, to the exclusion of activities on such a small scale as to be regarded as marginal and ancillary'.

ECJ *Lawrie-Blum v Land Baden-Wurttemberg*
66/85 [1986] ECR 2121

A British national was refused entry onto a teacher training course in Germany on national grounds alone. Germany rejected her claim that this breached her Art 39 rights to free movement of workers.

The ECJ held that she could be classed as a worker as she would receive a small salary as a trainee teacher and would be required to teach up to 11 hours per week. The level of pay and hours worked were not material in determining her status as a worker.

The ECJ stated that 'The essential feature of an employment relationship is that for a certain period of time a person performs services for and under the direction of another in return for which he receives remuneration'.

ECJ *Kempf v Staatssecretaris voor Justitie* 139/85 [1986] ECR 1741

A German national worked for 12 hours per week in Holland teaching music. His pay was too low to live on so he claimed supplementary benefit. His application for a work permit was rejected because his income was too low to support him.

The ECJ held that the mere fact that his income was so low that he required assistance did not prevent him from gaining rights under Art 39. He was entitled to the same benefits as Dutch nationals.

ECJ *Steymann v Statsecretaris voor Justitie* 196/87 [1988] ECR 6159

A member of a religious sect acted as a plumber for the group and received board and some 'pocket money' but no pay in return.

The ECJ held that he could be classed as a worker as he was engaged in a genuine and effective activity which was an inherent commercial aspect of his membership of the group.

ECJ *Hoekstra v Bestuur der Badrijfsvereniging voor Detailhandel en Ambachten* 75/63 [1964] ECR 177

A Dutch national fell ill while visiting her parents in Germany and sought to claim back the cost of treatment when she returned to Holland.

The ECJ held that she should succeed. The Court identified that the term 'worker' should be broadly interpreted and this should include a person who has lost a job but is capable of getting another.

This and the cases above demonstrate how broadly the ECJ is prepared to define the term 'worker'.

 ECJ *R v Immigration Appeal Tribunal ex p Antonissen* 292/89 [1991] ECR I-745

A Belgian national who had been resident in the UK and looking for work for two years challenged a deportation order following his conviction for possession of cocaine. Under UK law non-nationals could be deported after six months without work.

The ECJ held that work seekers were protected under Art 39 as much as those who had work. However, it also held that six months was an adequate time limit and would not be in breach of Art 39.

Procureur du Roi v Royer 48/75 [1976] ECR 497 p 69

ECJ | ***Bettray v Staatsecretaris van Justitie*** 344/87 [1989] ECR 1621

A German national, living in the Netherlands, was on a state sponsored drug rehabilitation scheme.

The ECJ held that he was not a worker as there was no genuine economic activity involved.

ECJ | ***Trojani v Le Centre Public d'Aide Sociale de Bruxelles*** C-456/02 [2004] All ER (EC) 1065

A French national moved to Belgium and lived in campsites and youth hostels. While resident in a Salvation Army hostel he received board and pocket money in return for completing various odd jobs as part of a personal socio-occupational reintegration programme.

The ECJ held that this activity was capable of falling within the scope of Art 39 but was for the national court to determine.

The Court said 'The national court must ascertain whether the services actually performed are capable of being regarded as forming part of the normal labour market'. It distinguished *Bettray*.

7.2 Workers and their families

ECJ *Diatta v Land Berlin* 267/83 [1985] ECR 567

A Senegalese woman and her French husband had settled in Germany and some time later separated. When she applied for renewal of her work permit she was refused on the ground that she was no longer a member of a worker's family.

The ECJ held that her rights under Regulation 1612/68 would not end until the marriage was lawfully terminated.

The ECJ recognised that 'if co-habitation of the spouses were a mandatory condition, the worker could at any time cause the expulsion of his spouse by depriving her of a roof'.

ECJ *Netherlands State v Anne Florence Reed*
59/85 [1986] ECR 1283

Reed, a UK national, went to join her partner, another UK national, who lived in the Netherlands. When she applied for a residence permit this was refused because she had not yet found work.

The ECJ held that, as a co-habitee, she could not come within the definition of worker's family in Art 10 of Regulation 1612/68 which referred to 'spouse'. However, the court did recognise that it was possible for a worker to have a co-habitee living with him as a 'social advantage' under Art 7(2) of the Regulation, since the same social advantage could be enjoyed by workers of the host state, and to deny this right to the migrant worker would be discrimination.

The definition of family in Art 10 is clearly narrow and has the potential to discriminate against certain relationships. This has been overcome by Directive 2004/38, the Citizens' Free Movement Rights Directive which repeals Art 10 of Regulation 1612/68. Article 2(2)(b) redefines 'family member' as including a 'partner [under] a registered partnership', taking into account civil marriages. Article 3(2)(b) also allows entry and residence rights to a partner 'with whom the EU citizen has a durable relationship'.

ECJ *Landesamt fur Ausbildungsforderung Nordrhein Westfalen v Gaal* C-7/94 [1995] ECR I-1031

Gaal was born in Belgium but brought up in Germany, later studying at a German university. At age 22 he applied for funding to study at a British university. German authorities rejected his claim since his father had died and he was not financially dependent on his mother.

The ECJ held that the definition of 'child' for the purposes of access to education under Art 12 of Regulation 1612/68 could not be subject to the same conditions of dependency as was the definition in Art 10 of the Regulation so Gaal could challenge the refusal.

The Court said 'to make the application of Art 12 subject to an age limit or to the status of dependent child would conflict not only with the letter of that provision, but also with its spirit'.

 ECJ *Centre Public d'Aide Sociale Courcelles v Lebon*
316/85 [1987] ECR 2811

Lebon was the child of French parents working in Belgium, was born in Belgium and had lived there for all but two years. On her return to Belgium, by which time her parents were retired, she was given income support but this was withdrawn on the basis that she was not seeking work. She was 24 at the time.

The ECJ identified that, while children of a worker cease to be classed as family on reaching 21, they do not lose family status if still dependent. Dependency does not cease merely because the child makes a claim for benefit. Otherwise this would mean that no member of a worker's family, other than a spouse and a child under 21, could ever make such a claim and remain a family member.

The Court stated 'The status of dependent ... is a factual situation ... and there is no need to determine the reasons for recourse to the worker's support or to raise the question whether the person is able to support himself by taking up paid employment'.

7.3 Rights of entry and residence, equal treatment and to remain after employment

Procureur du Roi v Royer 48/75 [1976] ECR 497

A French national was charged with entering Belgium illegally without a residence permit. He was refused the right to apply for a residence permit and given a deportation order with immediate effect, and with no right to appeal.

The ECJ held that the right of residence did not depend on the issue of a permit. Under the derogations in Directive 64/221, a migrant should have the same remedies as those for workers of the host state and it would be anomalous to make the procedural rights and safeguards conditional on the presence of a permit.

R v Pieck 157/79 [1980] ECR 2171 where ECJ held that, although Member States are entitled to penalise a migrant not complying with administrative formalities, this can never justify deportation. This is now incorporated in Art 9(3) of Directive 2004/38.

Commission v France (Re French Merchant Seamen) 167/73 [1974] ECR 359

French maritime law required that French merchant ships should hire crew members at a ratio of 3 French to 1 other nationality. The Commission challenged this law as in breach of Art 39.

The ECJ held that, despite the French argument that the law was no longer applied, it still breached Art 4(1) of Regulation 1612/68, guaranteeing equality in eligibility for employment and it would create an unacceptable ambiguity in the law if it was not repealed.

ECJ *Groener v Minister for Education* **397/87 [1989] ECR 3967**

A Dutch national applied for a teaching post in Ireland and was rejected because she did not have a Certificate of Proficiency in the Irish language as required for all Irish teachers. She challenged this as the teaching was to be in English.

The ECJ held that the Irish law was justified under Art 3(1) of Regulation 1612/68 since language was an important part of the culture of any state and there was no discrimination as the same requirement was made of Irish nationals who may not have the required proficiency in the language either.

ECJ *Wurttembergische Milchvertung-Sudmilch A.G. v Ugliola* **15/69 [1969] ECR 363**

A German employer, in determining the seniority of staff, took into account periods of national service in Germany. Ugliola completed national service in Italy which was not taken into account.

The ECJ held that this was a breach of Art 7(1) of the regulation; requiring that migrant workers must not be subject to differences in conditions, pay dismissal etc to the workers of the host state.

CJ *Sotgiu v Deutsche Bundespost* 152/73 [1974] ECR 153

The German post office paid a separation allowance for workers who were forced to live away from their families. This was 10DM for those whose family home was in Germany but only 7.5 DM for those whose family home was elsewhere.

The ECJ held that German nationals were much more likely to qualify for the higher allowance so the measure was discriminatory.

CJ *Firorini v SNCF* 32/75 [1975] ECR 1085

The widow of an Italian railway worker who had worked in France for SNCF was denied special fare reductions granted to large families. The French restricted rights to social advantages to those gaining them within employment and the widow had never worked.

The ECJ held that Art 7(2) of Regulation 1612/68 covered all social and tax advantages, whether gained through employment or not. These rights continued after the worker's death and it would be discrimination on nationality to deny them to the widow.

The ECJ rightly recognised that Art 7 cannot be interpreted narrowly otherwise it would promote inequality.

 ECJ *Gul v Regierungspresident Düsseldorf* 131/85 [1986] ECR 1573

A Cypriot national, with Turkish medical qualifications, married an English woman working in Germany. He had long term temporary work as an anaesthetist, gained German qualifications and applied to practice medicine in Germany but was refused on his nationality.

The ECJ held that Art 11 of Regulation 1612/68 gave family members the right to employment on the same basis as nationals and as such the only requirement was that he had the appropriate qualifications, which he did. The refusal was discrimination.

 ECJ *Michel S v Fonds national de reclassement des handicappes* 76/72 [1973] ECR 457

The mentally handicapped son of an Italian national employed in Belgium before his death was denied a benefit for people whose job prospects were affected by handicap.

The ECJ held that Art 12 of the Regulation entitled non-nationals to the same educational benefits as nationals including rehabilitation benefits.

Casagrande v Landeshauptstadt Munchen
9/74 [1974] ECR 773

The son of a deceased Italian who had worked in Germany
was refused an educational grant.

The ECJ held that Art 12 entitles the children of migrant
workers not only to the same access to education as nationals
of the host state but also to measures that support education
such as grants.

GBC Echtemach and Moritz v Netherlands Minister for
Education 389/87 & 390/87 [1989] ECR 723

In joined references Moritz, a German national, went to live
in the Netherlands with his father who worked there, rather
than remain with his mother. They then returned to Germany
but the son applied to complete his education in the
Netherlands and was refused.

The ECJ held that his access to education under Art 12 of the
regulation was not diminished by his father's return to
Germany.

Forcheri v Belgian State 152/82 [1983] ECR 2323

The wife of an Italian EC official in Belgium gained a place
on a social work training course but was required to pay a
'minerval' as all non-nationals were.

The ECJ held that, since she was legally resident in Belgium, the imposition was a breach of Art 12, discrimination on nationality.

The decision could also be seen as arising out of her status as the spouse of a worker under Regulation 1612/68.

ECJ *Lair v Universitat Hanover* 39/86 [1989] ECR 3161

A French national had worked intermittently in Germany with periods of voluntary unemployment. She gained a place to study languages and literature at Hanover University but her application for a maintenance grant was rejected because of a rule, only applied to non-nationals, that she had not worked for a complete five year period prior to the application.

The ECJ held that she was still a worker and under Art 7(1) of the Regulation was entitled to the same funding as nationals.

ECJ *Bosman v Royal Belgian Football Association and EUFA* C- 415/93 [1995] ECR I-4921

Bosman, a professional footballer with Liege FC in Belgium, was prevented from joining a new football club in France after expiry of his contract because of UEFA rules, which meant that he could not transfer without Liege receiving a fee from the French club. Liege set this too high for the French club to agree to and in effect prevented Bosman from working.

The ECJ held that the imposition of transfer fees for out of contract players was an unjustifiable restriction on their Art 39 rights.

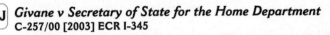

The ruling has had a major impact on the transfer system and also on the numbers of non-nationals playing in national leagues.

ECJ *Givane v Secretary of State for the Home Department*
C-257/00 [2003] ECR I-345

A Portuguese national lived and worked in the UK for three years before leaving for India for 10 months and returning to the UK with his Indian wife and three children. He died 21 months later. UK authorities refused the family the right to remain after his death because he had not resided continuously for at least two years.

The ECJ held that the right under Regulation 1251/70 must refer to the period immediately preceding the worker's death and could not be applied to the former period. This was because the rule was intended to establish a significant connection between the worker and his family and the state and to ensure a level of integration.

7.4 Derogations under Art 39

ECJ *Van Duyn v The Home Office* 41/74 [1974] ECR 1337

 A Dutch national and member of the Church of Scientology was offered a position in the Church in the UK but was refused entry by immigration officials on the grounds that the government had declared members of the church as undesirables, although the Church was not banned in the UK. They argued that her rights were exempted under the derogation in Art 39(3) and Directive 64/221.

 The ECJ recognised that the derogations of public policy and public security must, according to Art 3(1) of the directive, be based exclusively on the personal conduct of the individual concerned, but that membership of an organisation may constitute personal conduct. However, the Court did distinguish between past and present membership. It added that personal conduct can be sufficient to justify either deportation or refusal of entry.

 The decision is significant in that it gives Member States the means to legally expel people who are members of terrorist groups.

ECJ *Rutili v Ministere de l'Interieure* 36/75 [1975] ECR 1219

An Italian political activist was restricted in his movement by an order of the French Minister and challenged this order.

The ECJ held that, in order for the derogation of public policy to apply the individual must constitute a genuine and serious threat. Also the grounds for the restriction on movement must be indicated in a clear and comprehensive statement so that the person can prepare an adequate defence to the decision.

CJ *R v Bouchereau* 30/77 [1978] ECR 1999

A French national working in the UK was convicted of possession of drugs and given a suspended sentence. He was later charged again for possession and the magistrate contemplated a recommendation for an immediate deportation order.

The ECJ held that deportation, using the public policy or public security derogations was permissible only if the person posed a genuine and serious threat to society.

The Court held that 'The existence of a previous criminal conviction can … only be taken into account in so far as the circumstances which gave rise to that conviction are evidence of personal conduct constituting a present threat to the requirements of public policy'.

ECJ *Bonsignore v Oberstadtdirecktor of the City of Cologne*
67/74 [1975] ECR 297

An Italian national working in Germany accidentally shot his brother. He was convicted of illegal possession of a firearm and was ordered to be deported.

The ECJ held that deportation could not occur using the derogation as justification merely in order to act as a deterrent.

ECJ *Adoui and Cornaille v Belgian State*
115/81 & 116/81 [1982] ECR 1665

Two French women were employed as waitresses in a bar in Belgium and were also prostitutes. They were refused residence permits because it was shown that they sat in windows semi-naked.

The ECJ held that public policy only applies if Member States take similar repressive measures against their own nationals for similar behaviour. Since similar behaviour was only subject to small fines for nationals the derogation was being applied disproportionately.

7.5 The public service exemption

 ECJ

Commission v Belgium (Re Public Employees)
149/79 [1980] ECR 3881

A Belgian law reserved posts in the public service for Belgian nationals. The law included posts as diverse as nurses and plumbers employed by local authorities.

The ECJ held that the public service in Art 39(4) could not apply. This was reserved for posts involving the exercise of public authority in order to safeguard the general interests of the state.

➡

Commission v France (Re French Nurses) 307/84 [1985]
ECR 1725

CHAPTER 8

ARTICLE 43 AND RIGHTS OF ESTABLISHMENT AND FREEDOM TO PROVIDE SERVICES

Reyners v The Belgian State (1974)
Art 43 is directly applicable, so no need to introduce Directives and can be directly effective – and the case succeeded because of Art 12 no discrimination based on nationality
Gebhard v Milan Bar Council (1995)
National measures must be proportionate to the object to be achieved

RIGHTS OF ESTABLISHMENT
PROVISION OF SERVICES, RECEIVING SERVICES

Freedom to provide services
Van Binsberven v Bestuur van de Bedrijfsvereniging voor de Metaalnijverheid (1974)
Art 49 is directly effective so migrants are subject to the same rule as nationals
Luisi and Carbone v Ministero del Tesoro (1984)
The right is to receive as well as to provide services
SPUC v Grogan (1991)
But the right requries an economic element

8.1 Freedom of establishment and the problem of qualifications

ECJ *Reyners v The Belgian State* 2/74 [1974] ECR 631

Reyners was a Dutch national, resident in Belgium and qualified to practice Belgian law. He was being prevented from joining the Belgian bar because of a law requiring practicing lawyers to be Belgian nationals. Belgium was arguing that, since Art 43 was to be implemented by the introduction of 'sectoral' Directives, it failed the third test from *Van Gend en Loos*, it was conditional, and therefore not directly effective and could not be relied upon or enforced.

The ECJ held that, since Member States were to eliminate barriers to rights of establishment by the end of the transitional period, which had passed, and since Art 43 was sufficiently clear and precise, it was directly effective. Besides this, the measure was a straightforward breach of the requirement in Art 12 for there to be no discrimination based on nationality.

ECJ *Thieffrey v Conseil a l'Ordre des Avocates a la cour de Paris* 71/76 [1977] ECR 765

A Belgian national with a doctorate in law who had also practiced in Belgium had his qualifications accepted by a French university which awarded him the necessary Certificate of Aptitude for practice as a lawyer in France. However, the Paris Bar rejected his application on the basis that he did not have a French law degree.

The ECJ held that, following *Reyners*, this was a breach of Art 43, despite the fact that there was no harmonising Directive on professional legal qualifications at that time.

 ECJ *Patrick v Ministre des Affaires Culturelles*
11/77 [1977] ECR 1199

An English architect wished to establish in France but was prevented from doing so. Again there was no harmonising Directive for the profession. However, a French Ministerial Decree of 1964 had recognised the English qualifications as corresponding to the French ones.

The ECJ held that the refusal to deny Patrick a right to establish was purely discrimination based on nationality and breached Art 43.

 ECJ *Steinhauser v City of Biarritz* 197/84 [1985] ECR 1819

A German artist who was resident in France was prevented from exhibiting paintings in a crampotte (a fisherman's hut). A local law stated that the huts could only be rented by French nationals.

The ECJ held that, even though the law in effect gave advantages to French nationals rather than being an outright bar to establishment it was still direct discrimination and breached Art 43.

CJ *Paris Bar Council v Klopp* 107/83 [1984] ECR 2971

A German national, and member of the Dusseldorf Bar, applied for membership of the Paris Bar, wishing to set up chambers there as well as in Germany. He was rejected because of Paris Bar Council rules requiring avocats to establish chambers in only one place, the justification being that the rule was necessary to ensure adequate contact between lawyer and client.

The ECJ concluded that the measure was not proportionate since both transport and communication links were efficient and effective and a less restrictive measure could have been employed instead.

The ECJ stated 'Such a restrictive interpretation would mean that a lawyer once established in a particular Member State would be able to enjoy the freedom ... to establish in another Member State only at the price of abandoning the establishment he already had.

CJ *Vlassopoulou v Ministerio fur Justiz* C-340/89 [1991] ECR I-2357

A Greek national, qualified to practice in Greece, gained work in a German law firm with authorisation to advise on Greek and EC law. When she applied to join the German Bar she was refused on the grounds of lack of appropriate qualifications.

The ECJ held that the German authorities were obliged to assess the equivalence of her Greek qualifications and to be given a reasoned decision for the refusal as well as the right to appeal.

Directive 89/48 which provides for 'mutual recognition' of qualifications of three years at HE level, while allowing adaptation tests or periods. Directive 2001/19 which requires an appeals process and recognition of qualifications gained in third states.

 Gebhard v Milan Bar Council C-55/94 [1995] ECR I-4165

The Milan Bar brought disciplinary proceedings against Gebhard, a German lawyer, for using the term 'avvocato', a title reserved for those possessing Italian legal, professional qualifications.

The ECJ held that, because of the amount of time he had spent in Milan, he had established himself there and was entitled to rely on Art 43. The national measures should be applied in a non-discriminatory manner, be justified by imperative requirements in the general interest, be suitable and proportionate to attain the objective. Since the measure was to protect clients from unscrupulous people who passed themselves off as qualified lawyers it was justifiable in the circumstances.

8.2 Provision of services and receiving services

ECJ *Van Binsbergen v Bestuur van de Bedrijfsvereniging voor de Metaalnijverheid* 33/74 [1974] ECR 1299

Dutch rules required lawyers to be habitually resident before they could practice. This prevented a legal adviser from representing his client when the client moved to Belgium.

The ECJ held that this infringed Art 49 rights of freedom to provide services in another Member State by depriving them of all useful effect. It would discriminate against foreign nationals who would be less likely to be permanently resident.

Article 49 means that a person wishing to offer professional services in another state, while not establishing, is subject to the same rules of professional conduct as professionals in the host state. The right to offer services can only be denied where there is an imperative reason of public interest. The case also identifies that Art 49 is directly effective in the same way as Art 43.

 Society for the Protection of Unborn Children (SPUC) v Grogan C-159/90 [1991] ECR I-4685

The Irish constitution recognised the right to life of foetuses and other law made abortion illegal, meaning that women wishing to have abortions were forced to travel elsewhere. Grogan, a student, published information on where female students could obtain abortions in London and when the

SPUC gained an injunction from the Irish High Court to prevent publication, he challenged the Irish law as being in breach of his Art 49 rights to provide services.

The ECJ avoided declaring on the issue of the compatibility of the Irish Constitution and Art 49 by stating that the link between the abortions and the information Grogan had given was too tenuous for his activity to be called a service. Besides this there was no economic activity involved so there was no breach of Art 49.

ECJ *Luisi and Carbone v Ministero del Tesoro*
286/82 and 26/83 [1984] ECR 377

Two Italian nationals were prosecuted under an Italian law making it illegal to take more than a set amount of money out of the country. Both had taken large sums elsewhere for purposes of tourism and one had also done so for medical treatment. They were fined the differences between the amounts they were allowed to take out of the country and the legal amount under Italian law. They challenged the law as being in breach of Art 49.

The ECJ held that an important corollary of the right to provide services was the right also to receive services, without which Art 49 would be ineffective. There was a breach of Art 49.

The Court stated that 'The freedom to provide services includes the freedom, for the recipient of services, to go to another Member State in order to receive a service there, without being obstructed … and … tourists, persons receiving medical treatment and persons travelling for the purpose of education or business are to be regarded as recipients of services'.

CJ *Gravier v City of Liege* 293/83 [1985] ECR 593

A French art student was accepted for a four year course at the academy in Liege in Belgium and refused to pay the *minerval* (a supplementary fee that was imposed on foreign students but not Belgian students) and claimed that the fee breached Art 12.

The ECJ accepted that the course could be classed as vocational training, bringing it within the scope of Art 12 and meaning that the foreign students were indeed being discriminated against.

Blaizot v University of Liege 24/86 [1988] ECR 379 in which the ECJ made basically the same point in respect of university courses which the state had challenged as being academic not vocational.

Belgium v Humbel 263/86 [1988] ECR 5365 where ECJ made it clear that while privately funded education is covered by Art 49, state funded education cannot be classed as vocational and is not.

Brown v Secretary of State for Scotland 197/86 [1988] ECR 3205 which held that maintenance grants fell outside the scope of Art 49.

CJ *Cowan v French Treasury* 186/87 [1989] ECR 195

Cowan, an English tourist, was assaulted and robbed on the French Metro in Paris. He applied for compensation from the French equivalent of the Criminal Injuries Compensation

Board but was denied because French law reserved this for only French nationals.

The ECJ held that, in effect, this law obstructed his right to move freely to France and receive services (tourism) so was a breach of his rights under Art 49.

Omega C-36/02 [2005] I CMLR 5

A German company operated a 'laserdome' (where customers shot at each other with laser guided guns aimed at 'laser tags' that they wore. It used equipment bought from a British company. Local police successfully applied for an order to ban the activity as it was contrary to a German constitutional law prohibiting 'acts of simulated homicide and the trivialisation of violence' in order to preserve respect for human dignity.

The ECJ held that the German law infringed the British company's Art 49 rights to provide services, but the law was justified under the Art 46 derogation of public policy, public security or public health.

CHAPTER 9

CITIZENSHIP

> **Micheletti v Delagacion del Gobierno en Cantabria** (1992)
> Dual nationality gives rights to citizenship
> **R v Secretary of State for the Home Department, ex p Kaur** (2001)
> But where there is no national citizenship possible then Art 17 does not apply
> **Baumbast v Secretary of State for the Home Department** (2002)
> Art 18 is directly effective
> **Zhu and Chen v Secretary of State for the Home Department** (2004)
> Primary carers have the right to reside with children with citizenship

CITIZENSHIP

 Micheletti v Delegacion del Gobierno en Cantabria
C-369/90 [1992] ECR I-4239

An individual born in Argentina to Italian parents and with dual nationality wished to set up as a dentist in Spain. Spanish authorities rejected his application as Spanish law deemed him to have the nationality of his country of birth.

The ECJ held that, as he had dual nationality, he was an EU citizen and could invoke rights under Art 43.

ECJ *Collins v Secretary of State for Work and Pensions*
C-138/02 [2004] 3 WLR 1236

An individual with dual American and Irish nationality applied for job seeker's allowance in the UK but was refused because he was not 'habitually resident' in the UK as required by enabling regulations. EU workers under Regulation 1612/68 and those with rights of residence under Directive 68/360 were exempt from the rule.

The ECJ held that, although a job seeker under *Antonissen* (1991), he was protected against discrimination on nationality by Art 12 as he was a citizen by virtue of Art 17. The 'habitual residence' requirement was discriminatory, although it was objectively justifiable.

ECJ *R v Secretary of State for the Home Department, ex p Kaur*
C-192/99 [2001] All ER (EC) 250

A Kenyan Asian gained UK citizenship under the British Nationality Act 1948 but did not fall under any category under the Immigration Act 1971 entitling UK residence. The British Nationality Act 1981 then gave her British Overseas Citizen status but again no right of residence. When she entered the UK she applied for right to remain and take up employment but was rejected by the Home Secretary. She sought judicial review on the basis of Art 17 and Art 18.

The ECJ held that she could not have EU citizenship purely on the basis of her British Overseas Citizen status since this would give her the right to travel freely through the EU and reside anywhere but the UK.

To give her EU citizenship would clearly have been illogical in the circumstances. It is plain that a person can only invoke Art 18 if they already have a right of residence in at least one Member State.

 ECJ *Grzelczyk v Centre Public d'Aide Sociale*
C-184/99 [2003] All ER (EC) 385

A French national studying in Belgium sought financial assistance so he could concentrate on his studies rather than support himself by part-time work. He was refused because of his nationality and challenged this on the basis of Art 18, the right of free movement.

The ECJ held that he had been discriminated against directly under Art 12 so the only question was whether he fell within the terms for granting the assistance. As a migrant student he should receive the same benefits as students from the host state, so was entitled.

 ECJ *Baumbast v Secretary of State for the Home Department*
C-413/99 [2002] ECR I-7091

A German national, his Colombian wife, his eldest daughter from a previous relationship, with dual German and Colombian nationality, and their youngest daughter, with only Colombian nationality lived in the UK for three years

with the German working or self-employed during that time.
He then took work in China and then in Lesotho. His wife
applied for indefinite leave to reside in the UK for herself and
her daughters but was refused as she was not an EU citizen
and her husband could no longer be classed as a worker as he
worked outside of the EU.

The ECJ held that Art 18 was directly effective and could be
relied on by citizens. The wife had rights of residence as
primary carer of the eldest daughter, an EU citizen by virtue of
her dual nationality.

The ECJ also identified that, though Art 18 was subject to
limitations, Member States should only apply these limitations
subject to other principles such as proportionality.

ECJ *D'Hoop v Office National de l'Emploi*
C-224/98 [2003] All ER (EC) 527

A Belgian national undertook secondary education in Belgium
and then undergraduate study in France. After graduating she
applied for a benefit normally paid to graduates of Belgian
universities who had also completed school education in
Belgium and was refused because of her schooling in France.

The ECJ held that the rule was discrimination on nationality
contrary to Art 12 and that she could rely on her citizenship
rights under Art 18 and receive the allowance.

ECJ *Zhu and Chen v Secretary of State for the Home Department*
C-200/02 [2004] 3 WLR 1453

A Chinese couple with one child wished to avoid Chinese law allowing only one child and to have another so, while six months pregnant, the woman moved to the UK and gave birth. Although the child was born in Northern Ireland, under Irish law any person born in any part of Ireland gained Irish nationality. She then moved to Wales and their right to residence was challenged by authorities.

The ECJ held that the child, having Irish nationality, was an EU citizen, so the mother was entitled to residence of unlimited duration as the child's primary carer.

The Court identified that 'A refusal to allow the parent, whether a national of a Member State or ... of a non-member country, who is the carer of a child ... to reside with that child in the host Member State would deprive the child's right of residence of any useful effect ... accordingly the carer must be [allowed] to reside with the child in the host Member State for the duration of the residence'.

Carpenter v Secretary of State for the Home Department C-60/00 [2003] QB 416 where the same principle was applied to the Filipino wife of a UK national providing services in other Member States as she cared for his children from his first marriage, to deport her would prevent him from running his business in breach of Art 49.

CHAPTER 10

ARTICLE 81 AND ARTICLE 82 AND EU COMPETITION LAW

Meaning of undertaking
FENIN v Commission (2003)
'a single organisation of personal, tangible and intangible elements, attached to an autonomous legal entity and pursuing a long term economic aim'

Art 81 and restrictive trade practices
Types of prohibited behaviour
IAZ International Belgium (1983)
Applying dissimilar conditions to equivalent transactions
Agreements covered by Art 81
AEG Telefunken v Commission (1983)
Must involve collusive behaviour
ICI Ltd v Commission (The Dyestuffs Case) (1972)
Concerted practices are – a form of co-ordination between enterprises that has not yet reached the point where it is a contract
Affecting trade between Member States
Belasco v Commission (1989)
Must be capable of constituting a threat direct or indirect, actual or potential, on the pattern of trade
Object or effect of preventing/restricting or distorting competition
Etablissements Consten and Grundig v Commission (1966)
The key issue is whether or not competition is affected
Societe Technique Miniere v Maschinenbau Ulm (1966)
But the ECJ try to apply the rules so as not to stifle enterprise and initiative

COMPETITION

Art 81 exemptions
ACEC v Berliet (1968)
Exempt because intermediaries gained, which benefited consumers and there were no restrictions going beyond these positive aims and no threat to competition.

Art 82 and abuse of a dominant position
Continental Can Co. v Commission (1973)
Dominance is the 'power to behave independently without taking into account their competitors, purchasers or suppliers because of their share of the market or … availability of technical knowledge, raw materials or capital, they have power to control production or distribution for significant part of products'.
United Brands v Commission (1978)
And is measured against the relevant product market and the relevant geographical market
Hoffman-la-Roche v Commission (1979)
Abuse is where the behaviour of the undertaking 'has the effect of hindering the maintenance of the degree of competition still existing in the market or the growth of that competition'.

10.1 The meaning of 'undertaking'

Spanish hospitals and other health care bodies grouped together collectively under the name SNS and purchased supplies from FENIN, a Spanish association made up of most of the firms marketing medical goods and equipment. SNS delayed payment for supplies and FENIN complained that this amounted to an abuse of a dominant position under Art 82 although the claim was rejected.

The CFI held that SNS was not an undertaking for the purposes of Art 81 and Art 82. A purchaser clearly could be classed as an undertaking if the purchases were then used in the context of an economic activity, but SNS was financed by social security contributions and offered a free service to the public.

The established definition of undertaking is 'a single organisation of personal, tangible and intangible elements, attached to an autonomous legal entity and pursuing a long term economic aim'. The CFI in *FENIN* refined this definition, identifying that there must be some form of economic activity, however marginal, for an entity to be seen as an 'undertaking' for the purposes of competition law.

10.2 Art 81 and restrictive trade practices

10.2.1 Types of prohibited behaviour

 IAZ v International Belgium and others v Commission
96/82 [1983] ECR 3369

Under Belgian law only washing machines and dishwashers that conformed to Belgian standards could be connected to the mains water supply. These standards were set in an agreement between the national association of water suppliers and a trade association to which certain major suppliers of washing machines and dishwashers were affiliated. This had the effect of disadvantaging those suppliers who were not affiliated to the trade association who complained as a result.

The ECJ held that this conformed to one of the five types of prohibited anti-competitive behaviour identified in Art 81 since it applied dissimilar conditions to equivalent transactions with other trading parties, placing them at a competitive disadvantage. The other obvious effect was that it provided advantageous conditions to suppliers belonging to the trade association.

 Commission and France v Ladbroke Racing Ltd
C–359 and 379/95P [1998] 4 CMLR 27

French law required that companies which engaged in off course totalisator betting should be in the control of the Pari Mutuel Urbain (PMU). Ladbrokes argued that the agreements between those companies and PMU breached Art 81.

The ECJ held that there was no breach since the companies and PMU were operating according to national law. For the agreement to breach Art 81 it would require autonomous behaviour by the undertakings. As a result there could be no breach of Art 81 where national law imposed the agreement on the undertakings.

10.2.2 Agreements covered by Article 81

 AEG Telefunken v Commission 107/82 [1983] ECR 3151

A company refused to admit a trader to its distribution network and the Commission challenged this as being in breach of Art 81.

The Court rejected the argument that there was no agreement between undertakings. It held that this was because the refusal formed part of a system of contracts with the existing distributors.

An agreement between undertakings must always carry with it some form of collusion to distinguish from purely unilateral acts.

 ACF Chemiefarma v Commission (The Quinine Cartel Case) 41, 44, 45/69 [1970] ECR 661

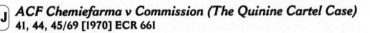

Firms in France, Germany and the Netherlands agreed to sales quotas on quinine and not to manufacture synthetic quinine.

This was challenged by the Commission as in breach of Art 81.

The Court held that there was a breach of Art 81. The agreement had been reached in order to artificially raise the price of the product by limiting its availability and prevent undertakings outside of the agreement from entering the market. It fell under the second type of prohibited agreement under Art 81(1), limiting or controlling production, markets, technical development or investment.

ECJ *ICI Ltd v Commission (The Dyestuffs Case) 48/69*
[1972] ECR 619

The major manufacturers of dyestuff, which represented more than 80% of sales of dyestuff, all raised their prices at exactly the same time. The Commission concluded that there had been a concerted practice and imposed fines on the undertakings. The undertakings challenged this decision and argued that there was no formal agreement, but merely parallel behaviour in an oligopoly (similar to a monopoly but where the majority of a market is controlled by a few undertakings rather than a single body).

The ECJ held that it was irrelevant that there was no formal agreement because collusion was identifiable in a series of Telex's to subsidiary companies all phrased in the same manner. There was a concerted practice amounting to a breach of Art 81.

The Court defined concerted practice as 'a form of coordination between enterprises that has not yet

> reached the point where it is a contract in the true sense of the word, but which, in practice, consciously substitutes co-operation for the risks of competition'. It added that '[it] may ... arise out of coordination which becomes apparent from the behaviour of the participants' and that, while 'parallel behaviour may not by itself be ... a concerted practice, it may, however, amount to strong evidence of such a practice if it leads to conditions of competition which do not correspond to the normal conditions of the market'.
>
> *Cooperatieve Vereeniging 'Suiker Unie' v Commission (The Sugar Cartel Case) 40-48, 50, 54-56, 111, 113, 114/73* [1975] ECR 1663

10.2.3 Affecting trade between Member States

 Vereeniging van Cementhandelaren v Commission
8/72 [1972] ECR 977

An agreement between cement dealers fixed the price of cement throughout the Netherlands. It was challenged by the Commission as being in breach of Art 81.

The Court held that the agreement was capable of affecting trade between Member States, even though the agreement was limited to the Netherlands, because it would strengthen existing divisions in the market and make penetration from other Member States more difficult, thereby protecting domestic industry.

ECJ *VBVB and VVVB v Commission* **43 & 63/82 [1984] ECR 19**

Dutch and Belgian booksellers operated a retail price maintenance agreement which was challenged successfully by the Commission.

The Court held that the agreement was one directly or indirectly fixing purchase or selling prices, identified as an anti-competitive practice in Art 81(1). It covered all books and all publishers and was not capable of exemption under Art 81(3) and so breached Art 81.

Publishers Association v Commission C-360/92P [1995] ECR I-23 where the ECJ held that the 'net book' pricing system in the UK was not in breach of Art 81 since it applied to certain books only and benefited the book trade in the UK and Ireland.

ECJ *Belasco v Commission* **246/86 [1989] ECR 2117**

Businesses in the Belgian roofing felt industry operated as a cartel and this was challenged as contrary to Art 81.

The Court rejected the argument that there was no affect on trade as the agreement was limited to sales in Belgium only. The agreement was capable of affecting trade between Member States as it placed competitors outside of the cartel at a disadvantage. There was a breach of Art 81.

10.2.4 The object or effect of preventing, restricting or distorting competition

Etablissements Consten and Grundig v Commission
56 & 58/64 [1966] ECR 299

Under an exclusive dealership agreement Consten was appointed sole distributor of Grundig's electrical goods in France in return for accepting that it would not import or export Grundig's products in any other EU country. Another company, UNEF, then sold Grundig's goods in France in breach of Consten's exclusive rights. Consten complained to the Commission and UNEF counterclaimed that the dealership was a breach of Art 81. The Commission issued a decision on this basis. Consten and Grundig argued that the agreement was for the purpose of streamlining distribution of Grundig's products in France where Grundig had competition from other manufacturers and was not an interference with trade.

The ECJ held that both vertical agreements (within the chain of production and distribution) and horizontal agreements (between competitors) were covered by Art 81. The exclusive dealership did breach Art 81 since it might affect trade between Member States by putting other businesses at a competitive disadvantage. It was irrelevant whether trade had been affected; it was sufficient that the agreement was intended to stifle competition.

ECJ *Societe Technique Miniere v Maschinenbau Ulm (the STM case)* 56/65 [1966] ECR 337

Under an exclusive supply agreement STM was given sole rights to sell Maschinenbau's heavy earth moving equipment in France. In contrast to *Consten & Grundig,* there was no agreement for exclusive use of the trademark, nor was there a ban on parallel imports or exports. The question for the ECJ was whether the agreement was capable of preventing, distorting or restricting competition.

The Court held that since the agreement was clearly only made because it was necessary to enable a firm penetration of the goods in a new market, and was therefore aimed purely at business efficiency, it did not breach Art 81.

The case is important because the Court also listed factors to be taken into account in deciding whether an agreement is capable of restricting, preventing or distorting competition:

- the nature and quantity of the product;
- the position and size of the undertakings in the market;
- the relationship with other agreements;
- the extent of the agreement;
- the link to parallel imports or exports.

ECJ *Frans Volk v Etablissements Vervaecke Sprl* 5/69 [1969] ECR 295

In an agreement between a Dutch electrical goods distributor (Vervaecke) and a German washing machine manufacturer (Volk), the Dutch firm gained exclusive distribution rights of the German company's washing machines in Belgium and Luxembourg. In return it agreed to a ban on parallel imports of Volk's products by third parties, a total protection for the German company.

The ECJ accepted that, since Volk only produced between 0.2% and 0.5% of washing machines in Germany and sold considerably fewer in Belgium and Luxembourg, the agreement could not be said to have any real effect on competition, the *de minimis* principle applied and there was no breach of Art 81.

This is now covered by the Commission Notice on Agreements of Minor Importance 2001 C368/13 with limits of total market share of 10% for horizontal agreements and 15% for vertical agreements.

10.3 Exemptions from Art 81

Com *Re Vacuum Interrupters* (Decision 77/160) [1977] 1 CMLR D67

Different manufacturers of switchgear engaged in a joint venture for the development of vacuum interrupters and applied to the Commission for exemption under Art 81(3).

The Commission issued a decision exempting the agreement since it met all four requirements of Art 81(3). It improved production and promoted technical progress since it made research possible. It would benefit consumers, did not impose unnecessary restrictions, and would not eliminate competition since the market stretched well beyond the EU and the undertakings faced significant competition from both the USA and Japan.

 ACEC v Berliet (Decision 68/39) [1968] CMLR D35

Two French manufacturers agreed jointly on the production of a prototype bus and applied for exemption under Art 81(3).

The Commission granted exemption since a benefit was gained by intermediaries in the distribution network which would ultimately benefit consumers. There were no restrictions going beyond these positive aims and no threat to competition.

10.4 Art 82 and abuses of dominant positions

 Continental Can Co. v Commission
6/72 [1973] ECR 215

Continental Can, a US multinational, through its European subsidiary, Europemballage, had an 86% share in Schmalbach, another company. Schmallbach had a dominant position in Germany in the market for tins for meat and fish products and for metal lids for glass containers. Europemballage then proposed a takeover of a Dutch packaging firm, Thomassen, and this was challenged as being a breach of Art 82. The Commission held that it was an elimination of potential competition and reduced consumer

choice, and so was an abuse of a dominant
position.

The ECJ overturned the Commission's Decision
on the ground that the Commission had failed to
identify the relevant product market and therefore
had not in fact proved dominance.

The Court defined dominance as 'power to behave
independently without taking into account their
competitors, purchasers or suppliers because of
their share of the market or ... availability of
technical knowledge, raw materials or capital, they
have power to control production or distribution
for significant part of products'.

 Com *Re Italian Flat Glass Cartel* (Decision 89/93) [1992] 5 CMLR 120

A group of undertakings enjoyed between 79% and 95% share
of the market for production of 'flat glass' and were challenged
when they engaged in concerted price fixing.

The Commission accepted that this was a dominant position
and that Art 82 could be invoked.

ECJ *United Brands v Commission* 27/76 [1978] ECR 207

 United Brands was one of the largest producers of bananas in the world, handling 40% of EC trade at the time. It was charging different prices in different Member States for the same goods. When this was challenged as being in breach of both Art 81 and an abuse of its dominant position under Art 82, United Brands argued that the relevant product market was fresh fruit, in which case it would have only a very small market share and dominance would not be an issue. The Commission argued, and it was accepted, that there was in fact a separate product market for bananas. This was because it was shown that bananas had a very specific market usually being consumed by the sick, the aged and the young. They could not therefore be considered merely as a part of a much more general market.

The ECJ held that there was a breach of Art 82 and considered again the definition of dominance. This involved considering both the relevant product market and the relevant geographical market and market share. The market share for bananas enjoyed by the company in Europe was between 40% and 45% which was held to be a dominant position. However, as the ECJ noted where the market share is less than 50% other factors must be considered, including the share of the nearest competitors. The two closest competitors in trade of bananas held 16% and 10% of the market.

 ECJ, building on its definition in *Continental Can,* identified that dominance is 'a position of economic strength ... which enables it to prevent

competition being maintained on the relevant
market by giving it the power to behave to an
appreciable effect independently of its competitors,
and ultimately its consumers'.

The case identifies that market share alone is not
conclusive evidence of dominance. United Brands
owned its own fleet and could control the volume
of other imports. The rest of the market was also
highly fragmented. There was reasonably healthy
competition in the relevant market but not enough
to prevent United Brands being able to act
independently of its competitors.

 NV Nederlandsche Baden-Indutrie Michelin v Commission
322/81 [1983] ECR 3461

The company supplied tyres for heavy earth moving vehicles
and offered bonuses to dealers for marketing effort but with
no clear basis for calculation. The Commission challenged this
as being an abuse of a dominant position.

The Court accepted that there was a distinct product market
since there was nothing to link the product to tyres in general.
It also accepted that the Netherlands could be the relevant
geographical market because of the effect on competition
since, by contrast to competitors, the company possessed not
only advanced technology but had a history of supplying such
specialist products.

ECJ *Hilti v Commission* T-30/89 [1990] ECR II-163

A firm was the dominant supplier of nail cartridges for its nail guns and was challenged by the Commission on the conditions it imposed. The Commission rejected the argument that there was cross elasticity of supply between nail guns and power drills.

The Court, in deciding that there was a breach of Art 82, accepted that the nail guns were a discreet product market and also that the relevant geographical market was the whole of the EC because of the ease and small cost of transporting the nail cartridges.

ECJ *Hoffman-la-Roche v Commission* 85/76 [1979] ECR 461

Hoffman La Roche offered loyalty rebates to purchasers of its vitamins and this was challenged as being in breach of Art 82. The company enjoyed a market share in the relevant product amounting to more than 80%.

The ECJ held that there was an obvious position of dominance in view of market share and also an obvious disadvantage to their competitors amounting to an abuse, so there was a breach. The Court also identified that relevant product market includes not only the product itself but other products that could be substituted for it.

On dominance the Court held 'such a position does not preclude some competition but enables [it] ... if not to determine, at least to have an appreciable effect on the conditions in which that competition will develop, and in any case to act largely in disregard of it'. It also defined abuse as 'an objective concept relating to the behaviour of an undertaking which is such as to influence the structure of the market where, as a result of the very presence of the undertaking in question, the degree of competition is weakened, and which, through recourse to methods different from those which conditions normal competition in products or services on the basis of the transactions of commercial operators, has the effect of hindering the maintenance of the degree of competition still existing in the market or the growth of that competition'.

CFI **_Tetra Pak International v Commission (No 2)_**
T-83/91 [1994] ECR II-755

The firm invented a process for filling cartons that would prolong the shelf life of the foodstuff to six months. It then refused to sell the machines for the process unless customers also bought the cartons (tetra paks) from its subsidiary company.

The Court accepted that there was no interchangeability of product so that the packaging was a relevant product market. It also held that the additional requirement in the contract was an abuse. It was making the completion of contracts subject to supplementary obligations that had no connection with the main contract.

ECJ *AKZO v Commission* C-62/86 [1986] ECR 1503

A company that enjoyed a dominant position in the benzole peroxide market cut its prices over a long period of time. It did so in order to put a small British competitor out of business.

The Court held that using price reductions to prevent competition did amount to an abuse. Any instance of directly or indirectly imposing unfair purchase or selling prices would amount to abuse.

ECJ *Magill TV Guide & ITP v Commission* C-241/91 P [1995] ECR I-743

Television companies which were the sole source of TV listings refused to supply the information to companies producing weekly listings for all channels, and the practice was challenged.

The Court held that the refusal was only to protect the company's own publications. There was a market for the product and the refusal therefore was to the prejudice of consumers and amounted to an abuse and a breach of Art 82.

 ECJ *Hugin Kassaregister AB v Commission* 22/78 [1979] ECR 1869

A Swedish firm manufacturing cash registers refused to supply spare parts to an English company which serviced and repaired such machines only in the UK. The Commission argued that this breached Art 82.

The Court accepted that there was a discreet relevant product market for the goods. However, it held that the abuse did not affect trade between Member States since it did not prevent the English company from operating in other Member States and Sweden was not at the time in the EU.

CHAPTER 11

EU DISCRIMINATION LAW

Equal pay
Defrenne v SABENA (1976)
Art 141 is directly effective
Bilka-Kaufhaus v Karen Weber Von Harz (1986)
Can only have differential pay rates if there is an 'objective justification':
- corresponds to genuine need of enterprise
- suitable for obtaining objective pursued by the enterprise
- necessary for that purpose

Barber v Guardian Royal Assurance Group (1990)
Pay is defined broadly in Art 141 and includes any benefit an employee obtains by reason of the relationship with the employer
Rummler v Dato-Druck GmbH (1986)
For claims of equal pay for work of equal value job evaluation schemes must not apply different criteria to men and women
Murphy v An Bord Telecom Eireann (1988)
Only equal pay can be awarded by the court even if work shown to be of superior value

Equal access
Johnston v RUC (1987)
Derogation is permitted for activities where sex is a determining factor or for the protection of women
Kalanke v Frei Hausestadt Bremen (1995)
But positive discrimination is not allowed
Webb v EMO (Air Cargo) (1992)
Dismissal on grounds of pregnancy is discriminatory and a breach of Directive 76/207
Dekker v Stichting (1990)
As is refusal to employ on the same grounds
Marshall v Southampton AHA (1986)
As is applying unequal retirement ages

DISCRIMINATION

The new anti-discrimination agenda
Prais v The Council (1976)
Freedom of religion was accepted as an essential principle of EC law and is now covered by the 'framework Directive'
P v S (1996)
And unequal treatment of transsexuals has been held to be based on their sex and is therefore discriminatory and in breach of EC law

11.1 Art 141 and equal pay

ECJ *Defrenne v SABENA (No 2)* 43/75 [1976] ECR 455

Defrenne was employed as an air stewardess with the Belgian airline and was paid significantly less than male cabin crew. She was unable to claim equal pay under Belgian law as there was no legislation on equal pay. She tried to bring an action under Art 141 and the Belgian authorities argued that the Art only affected the state and gave no rights to individuals.

The Court held that, since the Art complied with all of the *Van Gend en Loos* criteria for direct effect, in the absence of appropriate national law she could use the Art as the basis of her claim for equal pay. It also identified that the Art was both vertically and horizontally directly effective so could be used against private individuals as well as the state.

The Court stated that the prohibition on discrimination in pay 'applies not only to the actions of public authorities but also extends to all agreements which are intended to regulate paid labour collectively, as well as to contracts between individuals'.

Unfortunately, following representations from the UK and Ireland, the Art was held to be only prospectively, not retrospectively directly effective, meaning that many women lost out on potential and justifiable claims in those countries.

ECJ *Allonby v Accrington and Rossendale College*
C–256/01 [2004] 1 CMLR 35

The college dismissed all of its part time lecturers, two thirds of whom were women, before rehiring them through an agency. They were then paid less and lost other benefits, including pension rights. One of the women brought an action under Art 141 naming one of the male full timers as a comparator.

The Court held that there was no possible action under Art 141 as the employers were now different rather than the same.

Lawrence and Others v North Yorkshire County Council C–320/00 [2002] ECR I-7325 where the same applied to cleaners working for tendered private companies.

ECJ *Macarthys Ltd v Smith* 129/79 [1980] ECR 1275

A stockroom manageress discovered that her male predecessor had received significantly higher wages for the job. She claimed equal pay and the English court held that there was no claim as there was no contemporaneous male in the same employment.

The ECJ held that comparison could be made with any male doing the same work for the same or an associated employer and there did not have to be contemporaneous employment.

What could not be done was to use a hypothetical male comparator, but this was not the case here. In his reasoned opinion, the Advocate-General also suggested that 'equal work' could include jobs with a high degree of similarity even if they were not exactly the same.

 ECJ *Bilka-Kaufhaus v Karen Weber von Harz*
170/84 [1986] ECR 1607

 Harz was employed by a large department store for 10 years full time and then part time. Only 10% of male employees worked part time in contrast to 27.7% of women. Harz complained about the occupational pension scheme, only available to employees who had worked full time for 15 of the last 20 years, and from which she was excluded. The store accepted that it deliberately discriminated against part time work but claimed this was for the genuine need of the business to discourage part time work because part timers were less likely to be prepared to work late afternoons and Saturdays.

The ECJ held that this could amount to indirect discrimination. Although the provision was neutral it could have a greater impact on women employees because of the ratio of part time male and female employees. The Court also held that occupational pension schemes could be classed as pay for the purposes of Art 141.

 The Court left it to national courts to decide whether there is a real need to apply different rules for part timers, identifying that there must be an objective justification for doing so. It also set the criteria for determining whether there is an objective justification:

> - the measure must correspond to a genuine need of the business;
> - it must be suitable for obtaining the objective;
> - it must be necessary for that purpose.
>
> In the event the national court decided that there was no objective justification for the discrimination.

11.2 The definition of pay

ECJ *Garland v BREL* 12/81 [1982] ECR 359

The claimant challenged the policy of her employer to offer concessionary travel rates to former male employees and their families on retirement but not to former female employees.

The ECJ held that the concession should be available on a non-discriminatory basis irrespective of the fact that it was not founded in contractual entitlement but was a mere perk.

Article 141(2) defines pay in broad terms as the 'ordinary basic or minimum wage or salary or any other consideration, whether in cash or in kind, which the worker receives directly or indirectly, in respect of his employment'. The definition is much broader than that in English employment law. Nevertheless, the Court was still prepared to give a generous interpretation of this broad definition.

Worringham & Humphries v Lloyds Bank Ltd
69/80 [1981] ECR 767

The bank made supplementary payments to male employees under the age of 25 towards contributions to an occupational pension scheme. It did not make the same concession towards female employees of the same age and was challenged by female employees as being in breach of Art 141.

The Court of Justice held that sums which are included within the calculation of an employee's gross salary which are used to directly determine the calculation of other benefits such as redundancy payment, family credit etc constitute pay for the purposes of Art 141. Since the subsidy was denied to women under the age of 25 in the context of the case this amounted to a clear breach of Art 141.

Art 141 was preferred in the case to Directive 75/117 since there was no problem in establishing the direct effect of a Treaty Article in contrast to the problems that occur in relation to Directives when the claim is against a private individual.

Rinner-Kuhn v FWW Spezial Gebaudereinigung GmbH & Co. KG 171/88 [1989] ECR 2743

A part-time office cleaner was denied sick pay by her employers. She successfully challenged German legislation that permitted employers to exclude employees working under 10 hours per week from sick pay entitlement.

The ECJ held that continued payment of employees during periods of sickness absence fell with the definition of pay in Art 141(2). On this basis any legislation allowing employers to discriminate globally against a particular group of employees, part-timers, who were shown to be predominantly female, was in clear breach of Art 141.

ECJ *Barber v Guardian Royal Assurance Group*
262/88 [1990] ECR I-8889

Barber was made redundant at the age of 52 and, while he was paid the statutory redundancy payment by his employer, the employer would not pay him an early retirement pension under the contracted out scheme because this was only available to men over the age of 55 when made redundant. In contrast women in similar circumstances were eligible for the early pension scheme at age 50. Barber challenged the rule as being in breach of Art 141.

The ECJ held that money paid out under such schemes were indeed pay for the purposes of Art 141 and so there was an unjustified breach of the Art in Barber's case. The ECJ also identified that the nature of the scheme was irrelevant. Occupational pension schemes would still come within the scope of Art 141 whether they were employer schemes which supplemented the State's retirement scheme (as in *Bilka-Kaufhaus* (1986)) or the so-called 'contracted out schemes', which acted in place of the State scheme as was the case here.

The Court stated that 'Although it is true that many advantages granted by an employer also reflect considerations of social policy, the fact that a benefit is in the nature of pay cannot be called into question where the worker is entitled to receive the benefit in question from the employer by reason of the existence of the employment relationship'.

Because of the potential effects on contracted out schemes the Court decided that its ruling would not be applied retrospectively. The case, in any case, led to a flood of preliminary rulings, mainly from the UK and the Netherlands, on the precise scope of Art 141 in the context of occupational pension schemes.

11.3 Directive 75/117 like work and work of equal value

ECJ *Jenkins v Kingsgate Clothing Ltd* 96/80 [1981] ECR 911

Part-time workers in the garment industry, who were predominantly female with only one male part-time worker, were paid at a rate 10% below that of full-time workers. They challenged this as being discriminatory and contrary to Art 141 and Directive 75/117.

In the reference, on the question of whether differences in pay rates between full-time workers and part-time workers could be discriminatory where the part-time workforce in a particular employment was predominantly female, the ECJ identified that there would be no breach of EC law provided that the differences in pay were objectively justified and were not related to discrimination based on sex. The Court added, however, that such differences in pay could be in breach where, taking into account the difficulties that might be experienced by women in arranging to work full-time hours, that the policy on pay could not be explained by factors other than discrimination on grounds of sex.

The Court also recognised that the mere fact that the group which is allegedly discriminated against on pay includes both men and women does not prevent there from being discrimination, otherwise a token male could always be used to defeat the women's claim. The Court also recognised the possibility of using economic arguments to justify apparent discrimination, for example where it would be uneconomic to use part-timers for the specific work.

 ECJ | *Handels-og Kontorfunktionaernes Forbund v Dansk Arbejdsgiverforening for Danfoss* 109/88 [1991] ECR 3199

The Danish Employees' Union challenged criteria set by the Danish Employers Association as they had been applied by an employer, Danfoss. The criteria for establishing pay rates included both flexibility and seniority but, while the minimum pay for each grade was the same for both men and women, nevertheless the average pay for women within each grade was lower than for that of men.

The ECJ held that, even though neutral criteria for setting pay might appear to be non-discriminatory, if such criteria could be shown to result in systematic discrimination this could only be because the employer applied the criteria in a discriminatory manner.

 Rummler v Dato-Druck GmbH 237/85 [1986] ECR 210

A female packer who had been graded by her employer under a job evaluation scheme at a point below that which she thought her work merited challenged the criteria used in the job evaluation scheme. These included the muscular effort, physical hardship and fatigue associated with the individual job.

The ECJ held that the criteria used in job evaluation schemes must not differ according to whether the job is carried out by a man or by a woman. It also stated that it must not be organised in such a manner that it has the practical effect of discriminating against one sex. The criteria must be objectively justified and to be so they must be appropriate to the tasks to be undertaken and also correspond to a genuine need of the business. Nevertheless, the Court also stressed that it would be possible to have criteria which included factors which favoured one sex over another provided that these criteria were part of an overall package which included factors that did not. In the scheme in question other criteria which were non-discriminatory included knowledge, training, and responsibility.

Although the Court focused on objective justification for particular criteria within an overall package that did not discriminate, in accepting physical strength as an acceptable criteria it does seem to be allowing employers to set criteria that would naturally discriminate against women and in favour of men.

 ECJ *R v Secretary of State for Employment, ex p Seymour-Smith and Perez* C-167/99 [1999] ECR I-623

Two women complained that the then two year qualifying period in English law for unfair dismissal rights unfairly discriminated against women because at any given time more women would fall within that period than men because of career breaks for child rearing.

The ECJ held that awards of compensation for unfair dismissal did count as pay for the purposes of Art 141. The Court considered that such compensation is a form of deferred pay which the worker is entitled to as a result of her employment, and that the sum in effect represented what the worker should have earned if the employer had not unlawfully terminated the employment relationship. The Court added that it was for the Member State to determine whether in fact there had been discrimination by deciding whether a significant number of women were indeed affected.

The Court stated that 'In order to establish whether a measure adopted by a Member State has disparate effect as between men and women to such a degree as to amount to indirect discrimination ... the national court must verify whether the statistics available indicate that a considerably smaller percentage of women than men is able to fulfil the requirement'.

ECJ *Murphy v An Bord Telecom Eireann* 157/86 [1988] ECR 673

A female skilled factory worker discovered that she and 28 colleagues were being paid less than a male employee, an unskilled store labourer. She challenged this in the national courts and, following a job evaluation study was informed that her work was actually of greater value than that of her male comparator and, since the work was of unequal value no equal pay claim was possible. The case was referred to the ECJ.

The ECJ held that despite the fact that Art 141 and Directive 75/117 referred to the principle of equal pay for work of equal value, this could not be used as a ground for justifying the discrimination or for dismissing her claim to equal pay in the circumstances.

The Court stated that 'to adopt a contrary interpretation would be tantamount to rendering the principle of equal pay ineffective ... an employer would easily be able to circumvent the principle by assigning additional or more onerous duties to workers of a particular sex, who could then be paid a lower wage'.

11.4 The equal treatment Directive

 ECJ *Johnston v Chief Constable of the Royal Ulster Constabulary* 222/84 [1987] QB 129

A female officer in the Royal Ulster Constabulary claimed that the policy of not issuing firearms to female officers was in breach of the right of equal treatment under Directive 76/207 and that the policy acted in effect as a bar to promotion for female officers. The RUC claimed that the policy was justified on grounds of public safety and national security and was also authorised by a statutory instrument. It also argued that to allow women to carry arms would increase their risk of becoming targets for assassination and that the derogation Art 2(2) of Directive 76/207 would apply. The Secretary of State for Northern Ireland issued Mrs Johnston with a certificate confirming the point conclusively.

The Court held that there was no general public safety exemption to the equal treatment principle in the Directive. It also stated that the only derogation available was that in Art 2 of the Directive, on occupational activities which by reason of their nature or the context in which they operate mean that the sex of the worker is a determining factor. It held that the derogation should be applied strictly but accepted that the principle of proportionality should also be applied. The policy could fall within the derogation because of the politically sensitive situation then in Northern Ireland.

The ECJ did recognise that the effect of the certificate was to deprive female officers of the right to a judicial hearing or indeed any remedy. As such it was a breach of human rights.

 Kalanke v Frei Hausestadt Bremen C-450/93 [1995] ECR I-3051

A male applicant for a post complained about the appointment of a female applicant where both had equal qualifications and the justification for the appointment was a

German law giving preference to female applicants where there was an under-representation of females at the level of the post in question.

The ECJ held that the exemption to promote equal opportunity and to remove existing inequality contained in Art 294) of Directive 76/207 could not apply. This was because the measure was for the purpose of the provision was to allow measures to eliminate actual instances of inequality, not to establish any absolute priority for women or positive discrimination.

The case caused uproar in certain quarters and there was some call for Art 2(4) to be extended to allow for positive discrimination in order to assist in removing current levels of inequality. However, subsequent case law that has distinguished from *Kalanke* would seem to have taken care of the problem.

Marschall v Land Nordrhein-Westfalen C-409/95 [1997] ECR I-6363 p125

 Marschall v Land Nordrhein – Westfalen
C-409/95 [1997] ECR I-6363

A male teacher, a German national, applied for a promotion in a comprehensive school in Germany but was rejected because there were fewer women than men in his particular career bracket and so a similarly qualified woman was given the post. The justification for the decision was under German law which provided that women with equal qualifications and suitability were to be given priority in such appointments unless reasons specific to an individual male candidate tilted the balance in his favour. The man challenged this 'positive discrimination' as being unlawful under Directive 76/207.

The ECJ distinguished *Kalanke* (1995) on the basis of this qualifying clause and held that such a clause made the measure non-discriminatory by contrast to those measures that merely confer automatic priority for women.

 ECJ *Dekker v Stichting Vormingscentrum voor Jong Volwassenen (VJV Centrum) Plus* C-177/88 [1990] ECR I-3941

A pregnant woman was refused employment because she was pregnant. She claimed this was direct discrimination. The company to whom she had applied for employment argued that there were no male candidates for the post so there could be no discrimination when they chose from an exclusively female file of candidates.

The ECJ rejected the company's argument and held that refusal to employ a woman because she was pregnant was directly linked to her sex and amounted to direct discrimination and was unjustifiable.

The Court stated that 'A refusal of employment on account of the financial consequences of absence due to pregnancy must be regarded as based, essentially on the fact of pregnancy [and] cannot be justified on grounds relating to the financial loss which an employer who appointed a pregnant woman would suffer for the duration of her maternity leave'.

ECJ *Webb v EMO Air Cargo* C-2/93 [1992] ECR I-3567

A female worker was appointed by a small business with only 16 employees to cover maternity leave for one of them. When she was taken on it was envisaged that she should be able to stay with the firm even after the end of the maternity leave that she was covering. After she had been in employment two weeks she found that she was pregnant and when her employer was informed she was promptly dismissed. She then brought a claim in a tribunal for unfair dismissal on the ground that the sole reason for her dismissal was her pregnancy and was therefore discriminatory.

The Court in the reference held that dismissal of a female worker in an indefinite period of employment solely for reasons of her pregnancy did amount to unlawful discrimination contrary to Directive 76/207. The question left open by the Court was whether the dismissal would be non-discriminatory and therefore lawful if the employment was for a definite period.

Jiménez Melgar v Ayuntamiento de Los Barrios C-438/99 [2001] ECR I-6915 and *Teledenmark v Handels-og Kontorfuntionaererernes Forbund i Danmark* C-109/00 [2001] ECR I-6993. In both cases the ECJ held that no distinction should be drawn between pregnant workers on indefinite contracts and those on temporary contracts.

ECJ *Burton v British Railways Board* 19/81 [1982] ECR 555

A railway worker wishing to retire at age 58 challenged his employer's voluntary redundancy scheme which was eligible to women at age 55 and men not until 60. Since this fell within an exemption in the Sex Discrimination Act 1975 his only possible claim was under Directive 76/207.

The ECJ held that the Directive applied in principle to access to voluntary redundancy schemes. However, as the ages for voluntary redundancy were calculated according to different statutory retirement ages for men and women which was permitted under Directive 79/7 then the claim under Directive 76/207 would fail.

11.5 The new anti-discrimination agenda

ECJ *Prais v The Council* 130/75 [1976] ECR 1589

A Jewish woman applied for a post as a Community official, not mentioning her faith in the application. When she had to sit an exam in support of her application on a specific date she then explained that this was impossible as it fell on an important Jewish festival. She was then prevented from completing the exam because the Council decided that it was necessary for all candidates to sit the exam on the same day. She challenged this decision.

The Court recognised that freedom of religion was an essential principle of EC Law and that people should not be disadvantaged because of their religion. However, the Court upheld the decision of Council since it had not been informed in advance of the difficulty which therefore prevented it from making the necessary arrangements to avoid the discrimination on religion.

ECJ *P v S* C-13/94 [1996] ECR I-2143

A male employee of a Cornwall college informed his Director of Studies that he was to undergo 'gender reassignment' to become a woman which would involve a period of dressing and behaving like a woman and would ultimately result in surgery for a full sex change. He was later dismissed and claimed that this was unlawful sexual discrimination and therefore a breach of Directive 76/207.

The question for the ECJ was whether dismissal of a transsexual was not for reasons of gender since it did not involve in effect a single gender. The Court held that the Directive could not be viewed in such a narrow way. The whole purpose of the Directive was to prevent discrimination and promote equality, in any case, a fundamental principle of law to be applied universally. It rejected the view submitted by the British Government that the dismissal was not discriminatory since it could have equally applied to a female to male transsexual. The transsexual was being discriminated against by being treated less favourably than a person of the sex to whom he/she had belonged prior to the gender reassignment.

ECJ *Grant v South West Trains Ltd* C-249/86 [1998] ECR I-621

An employer provided concessionary rail travel for its employees in respect of legal spouses and cohabitees of the opposite sex. Grant tried to claim concessionary travel on behalf of her lesbian partner and was rejected. She claimed that this was discriminatory.

The ECJ appeared to narrow to an extent the broad principle stated in *P v S*, although with sound reason. The Court held that the policy could not be discriminatory since it did not treat female workers differently, and therefore less favourably, than male workers. The provision in the contract would apply in the same way to male homosexuals so the discrimination was not based on sex.

This position is likely to change with the introduction of Art 13 in the Treaty of Amsterdam giving the Council the power to take action to remove discrimination on based on sex, race or ethnic origin, religion and belief, disability, age and sexual orientation. This has already been put into practice with the 'framework Directive'.

 ECJ *KB v National Health Service Pensions Agency* C-117/01 [2004] All ER (EC) 1089

Transsexuals could not marry under English law. The National Health Service Pension Scheme provided benefits for widows and widowers of members of the scheme but there was no provision for unmarried partners. This rule was challenged as discriminatory.

The ECJ held that the rules combined in this way constituted a breach of EC law and based its reasoning on recent cases in the European Court of Human Rights identifying that the rule preventing transsexuals from marrying breached Art 12 of the Convention.

ECJ *Hertz v Aldi Marked* 179/88 [1990] ECR I-3979

A part-time cashier was dismissed when she was repeatedly absent from work because of illness which, although connected to pregnancy and childbirth, actually occurred some time afterwards.

The ECJ held that, although under Art 10 of the Safety and Health at Work of Pregnant Workers Directive 92/85, a dismissal during pregnancy or maternity leave is prohibited, here it was impossible to say that the dismissal discriminated against her on grounds of her sex. This was because it was also impossible to distinguish between her illness at that time and any illness suffered by a man who might be subject to the same dismissal procedure.

It was obviously also crucial to the decision that the illness occurred between a year and two years after her maternity leave expired.

ECJ *Wippel* C-313/02 [2005] 1 CMLR 9

An Austrian employee was contracted on a 'work on demand' basis with no fixed hours or income. She was also able to refuse the work. Eventually she brought an action seeking to class herself as a part-time worker for the protections that this offered.

The ECJ held that it was for Member States to determine whether a particular worker was a part-timer and therefore within the scope of the Protection for Part-Time Workers Directive 97/81.

Under clause 2(2) of the Directive Member States may exclude part-time workers who are classed as casual. This has the effect of denying those workers the right to enforce clause 4(1) which requires that part-time workers should not be treated less favourably than full-time workers merely because they work part-time unless this can be objectively justified.

ECJ *SIMAP* C-303/89 [2000] ECR I-7963

During litigation between a Spanish doctors' union and the Health Ministry, the question arose whether time spent at home 'on call' counted towards working time for the purposes of determining the maximum weekly working time under Art 6 of the Working Time Directive 93/104 (now Directive 2003/88).

The ECJ held that while being 'on call' at the hospital did count towards the working week, being on call at home did not.

As the Court said this was because 'in that situation doctors may manage their time with fewer constraints and pursue their own interests'.

ECJ *Jaeger* C-151/02 [2003] ECR I-8389

A German doctor was required to spend part of his week 'on call'. This had to be spent at the hospital and he was only required to attend a patient when the need arose. When he was not needed he could sleep in a bedroom at the hospital. He argued that this 'on call' period should count towards his average weekly working hours, while his employer maintained that the time he spent in bed was his rest period.

The ECJ, applied *SIMAP* (2000), and held that, for the purposes of Art 3 of the Working Time Directive 93/104 (now Directive 2003/88) the entire period on call should count towards his working week.

The Court identified that 'The objective of [the Directive] is to secure the effective protection of the safety and health of employees by allowing them to enjoy minimum periods of rest'. It also acknowledged that in the case of junior doctors 'the periods during which their services are not required … may … be of short duration and/or subject to frequent interruption' and that they 'may be prompted to intervene … to monitor the condition of patients'.

Pfeiffer & Others C-397–403/01 [2005] 1 CMLR 44 where periods of inactivity of German Red Cross workers 'on call' during emergencies was not counted as working time in German legislation, which the ECJ held had incorrectly implemented the Working Time Directive.

R (on application of BECTU) v Secretary of State for Trade and Industry C-173/99 [2001] 1 WLR 2313

The Broadcasting, Entertainment, Cinematographic and Theatre Union (BECTU) alleged that its members were being unfairly denied paid annual leave contrary to Art 7 of the Working Time Directive 93/104 (now revised in the Working Time Directive 2003/88). Its argument was based on the fact that the majority of members were employed under short term contracts and under Regulation 13 of Working Time Regulations 1988 (which had implemented the Directive) annual leave entitlement only applied to employees of more than 13 weeks continuous service.

The ECJ, in one of the first references on the Directive, held that the UK had failed to properly implement the Directive by imposing conditional requirements for entitlement when there was nothing in the Directive permitting such a provision.

Gibson v East Riding of Yorkshire Council [1999] IRLR 359

A swimming instructor employed by a school was not required to work during the school holidays and received no wages for that time under her contract. She brought an action in an Employment Tribunal claiming that she was in effect being denied her right under Art 7 of the Working Time Directive to paid annual leave. The Tribunal held that her employer, the local council, was an emanation of the state for the purposes of vertical direct effect but that the provision was conditional and therefore failed the *Van Gend en Loos* (1963) criteria for direct effect.

The Employment Appeal Tribunal reversed this decision and held that the Directive was directly effective vertically so that the woman was entitled to paid leave.

INDEX